TALES FROM THE INDIANA HIGH SCHOOL BASKETBALL LOCKER ROOM

TALES FROM THE INDIANA HIGH SCHOOL BASKETBALL LOCKER ROOM

A Collection of the State's Greatest Basketball Stories Ever Told

Jeff Washburn
with Ben Smith

SPORTS
PUBLISHING

Sports Publishing books may be purchased in bulk at special discounts for sales promotion, corporate gifts, fund-raising, or educational purposes. Special editions can also be created to specifications. For details, contact the Special Sales Department, Sports Publishing, 307 West 36th Street, 11th Floor, New York, NY 10018 or sportspubbooks@skyhorsepublishing.com.

Sports Publishing® is a registered trademark of Skyhorse Publishing, Inc.®, a Delaware corporation.

Visit our website at www.sportspubbooks.com

10 9 8 7 6 5 4 3 2 1

Library of Congress Cataloging-in-Publication Data is available on file.

Cover design by Tom Lau
Cover photo credit: Associated Press

ISBN: 978-1-68358-136-9
Ebook ISBN: 978-1-68358-153-6

Printed in the United States of America

To my parents, Maxine and the late Paul "Sonny" Washburn, for introducing me to Indiana high school basketball when I was less than six months old, then driving me from our Lafayette home to countless games in tradition-rich cities such as Muncie, Anderson, New Castle, Richmond and Marion years before I was old enough to provide my own transportation.

To my wife, Cheryl, and our son, Jade Ryan, for understanding that the lifestyle of a sports writer/author certainly does not include a traditional eight-to-five, Monday-through-Friday schedule.

To my Lafayette Journal and Courier sports staff colleagues, for whom I have the greatest respect and admiration.

To my friend Bobby Plump and the "Hoosier Hysteria" miracle that was Milan's 1954 state championship, which was achieved during the year I was born.

And to all Indiana high school basketball players, coaches, administrators and fans who have enriched my life much more than any of them ever will know.

CONTENTS

INTRODUCTION

Order a cup of coffee at Billy Ann's in Bluffton, Bill's in New Castle or Bauer's in Loogootee, and chances are, one topic—Indiana high school basketball—will be discussed before the cream and sugar settle into the warm beverage.

Hoosiers reluctantly acknowledge that basketball was not invented in Indiana, but they are convinced the sport found a permanent home in high schools from South Bend in the north to North Vernon in the south, and everywhere in between.

This book—a compilation of *Tales* spanning a full century—is a snapshot of why the friendly people of this state take this sport oh so very seriously.

From early November through the state championship games in late March, Hoosiers rarely venture too far from the gymnasiums and fieldhouses that often dominate a community's landscape.

It often is said that religion, politics, sweet corn and basketball compose the core of Indiana. And not particularly in that order.

Indiana high school basketball is much more than a hobby or pastime. For many Hoosiers, it is a way of life. New Yorkers attend the theatre. Bostonians treasure their Red Sox.

In Indiana, Friday and Saturday nights are reserved for those 16-, 17- and 18-year-olds whose skills include tossing an orange ball through a round rim decorated with white twine.

And it has been that way since 1911, when Crawfordsville won Indiana's first high school basketball state tournament.

Tales weaves through Franklin, where the "Wonder Five" captured three consecutive state championships in 1920, '21 and '22, and on to Marion, where "Purple Reign" won three in a row some 65 years later—1985, '86 and '87.

Tales chronicles the life of Lebanon's Rick Mount, who probably is the greatest pure shooter this sport ever has known. Mount developed rock-hard wrists flinging a tennis ball through a Planter's Peanuts can.

Then there's Damon Bailey, the kid from Bedford-North Lawrence who became an Indiana basketball legend in eighth grade, when Bob Knight traveled to tiny Heltonville, Indiana, to watch him play.

Bailey capped a memorable four-year high school career as Indiana's all-time leading scorer. And yes, he won a state championship in his final high school game.

In Indianapolis, Oscar Robertson-led Crispus Attucks and George McGinnis-led Washington experienced unbeaten seasons and a state championship in their senior years. Big-city kids with big-city skills.

Tales is about Muncie Central, the purple-clad Bearcats whose eight state titles are more than any other Indiana high school.

Small-school powers Rossville, Waldron, Loogootee, Argos, Lafayette Central Catholic, Attica and Covington are front and center in *Tales*.

And of course, Milan, Bobby Plump and the cornerstone state championship "feel-good" story of 1954 are documented within the pages of this celebration of Indiana high school basketball.

The Milan story inspired the hit movie *Hoosiers*, which to this day is viewed by almost every small-town school's basketball team as it prepares for a big game—regular season or tournament.

When *Hoosiers* premiered in New York City, Lafayette native Mike Casey, a modeling agency executive whose father, Dan, was a member of Lafayette Jeff's 1948 state championship team, took a date to see the film.

"So what did you think?" Mike Casey asked the attractive New York-born woman.

"Cute, I guess, but I really don't get it ... a movie about high school basketball?" she replied.

Mike Casey never called the woman again.

Strange? In 49 other states, high school basketball is a game. In Indiana, it is a way of life. A passion. A treasure.

Come stroll through these pages, where Indiana schoolboys and schoolgirls come to life and grow into basketball legends beyond their wildest dreams.

CHAPTER 1

LEGENDS

An Idol's Idol

Long before his dominating UCLA teams were winning a record 10 NCAA tournament championships, John Wooden was an impressionable Indiana high school basketball standout at Martinsville High School.

The coach known nationally as "The Wizard of Westwood" during his days at UCLA may have selected a different career path had it not been for Indiana's 1926 state championship game staged in Indianapolis's Exposition Building.

Wooden, then a sophomore, led his team to the title game, where Marion and dominating 6-foot-7 center Charles "Stretch" Murphy were waiting.

Murphy, then a senior, paced Marion to a 30-23 victory, but Wooden learned more during that defeat than he ever could have learned in victory.

*John Wooden of the Martinsville Artesians was a star in the
late 1920s.*

"Stretch Murphy proved to me just how good a basketball player could be," said Wooden, who would team with Murphy in 1930 at Purdue University. "Until I witnessed Stretch Murphy's performance, basketball was something I simply enjoyed. Stretch made it an art form.

"My family had lived on a farm until my father took a job as a massage therapist at one of the artesian spas in Martinsville. I started playing basketball, and in 1926, my life changed forever."

Wooden, who passed away in 2010, just shy of his 100th birthday, led Martinsville to the 1927 state championship and to another second-place finish in 1928, this time a loss to Muncie Central.

After earning All-American honors at Purdue, Wooden entered coaching—first at the high school level, then at Indiana State before moving on to UCLA, where his record of excellence almost certainly never will be surpassed.

The Game That Inspired Hoosiers

Bobby Plump's Indianapolis-based insurance agency receives a large volume of daily phone calls seeking quotes for auto, family, home and life policies.

The office staff also receives plenty of calls seeking answers to questions such as, "How long did he hold the ball in the center of the court?" and "How long was that final shot?"

Four minutes and 13 seconds is the answer to Question No. 1, and approximately 15 feet is the answer to Question No. 2.

It has been more than 60 years since Plump's 15-foot jump shot with three seconds remaining lifted tiny Milan to a 32-30 victory against mighty Muncie Central in the 1954 Indiana high school state championship game, but the moment—for many Hoosiers—remains frozen in time.

So much so that the hit film *Hoosiers* is based on Milan's *Cinderella* run to Indiana's state crown, giving hope to every small school in this basketball-crazy state.

Ripley County-based Milan is approximately 30 miles from Cincinnati in southeastern Indiana. Milan's basketball teams won several sectional championships prior to 1953, but when Plump hit his stride during his junior season, he literally put the Milan Indians on the map.

They reached Indiana's Final Four in 1953, losing to eventual state champion South Bend Central in the semifinal round.

Plump flashed signs of things to come, scoring 19 points in that loss to South Bend Central.

When the 1953-54 season began, Milan figured to be a major player in the state tournament, but Muncie Central was loaded with talent and more athleticism than the Indians and figured to be the team to beat.

Sure enough, Milan fought its way through the sectional, regional and semistate, then beat Terre Haute Gerstmeyer to earn a state title game shot at Muncie Central.

Milan, whose population in 1954 was approximately 1,100, played a near-perfect first half for coach Marvin Wood, building a 25-17 lead through 16 minutes, despite poor shooting from Plump.

"Mr. Basketball"—He'll Lead The Hoosiers.

Bobby Plump as Mr. Basketball in 1954.
(The Indianapolis Star)

In the third quarter, Gene Flowers and Jimmy Barnes helped Muncie Central make its move, pulling the Bearcats into a 26-26 tie with eight minutes to play.

The Bearcats scored early in the fourth quarter, seizing a 28-26 advantage. At that point, Wood made one of the most unusual yet effective decisions in Indiana high school tournament history.

He ordered Plump to hold the ball at center court as he pondered his options. For the next 4:13, those watching and listening to this dramatic game couldn't believe what was taking place.

Milan trailed, yet the Indians were holding the ball. Years later, Wood acknowledged that he was unsure of the proper strategy and decided to take some time to think about it.

Finally, with just more than two minutes to play, he ordered Plump to shoot. The Milan star missed, but seconds later, fellow guard Ray Craft scored to tie it at 28.

A Muncie Central turnover gave the ball back to Milan, and Plump made two pressure-packed free throws. The Indians led 30-28. But Flowers's final basket pulled Muncie Central back into a tie at 30 with less than a minute to play.

Milan brought the ball across the 10-second line, and Wood called a timeout with 18 seconds to play. He told his players to inbound the ball to Plump, then get out of his way.

With ball in hand, Plump watched as the other four Indians gathered on the left side of the court, leaving him and Muncie Central defender Barnes one-on-one with the clock ticking down.

Plump made his move with five seconds to play, shooting just over Barnes's outstretched fingers. The ball eased through the bottom of the net, giving Milan the 32-30 victory that is still talked about from South Bend in the north to North Vernon in the south.

Milan finished the 1953-54 season with a 28-2 record, but victory No. 28 certainly is the one that forever will be remembered by those Hoosiers who adore Indiana high school basketball.

"I know it sounds crazy, but 50 years after that game, at least one person every day wants to talk about it ... me holding the ball and then making the shot," Plump said. "It's a wonderful story, but it's much more than just a story."

For Plump, it is a way of life.

The Big "O"

Oscar Robertson grew up in humble, inner-city surroundings, but during the 1954-55 and 1955-56 seasons, the 6-foot-5 guard carved an Indiana high school basketball legacy that still is revered more than sixty years later.

Green- and gold-clad Indianapolis Crispus Attucks was an African-American high school whose students were expected to embrace academics with the same passion they embraced basketball.

Under coach Ray Crowe's tutelage, the "Big O" was the model player and the model student.

*Oscar Robertson (left) with Indianapolis
Crispus Attucks coach Ray Crowe in 1956.*

During his junior and senior seasons, Robertson led the Crispus Attucks Tigers to a 62-1 record and back-to-back Indiana high school state championships.

As a junior, Robertson scored 30 points in a 97-74 title-game drubbing of Gary Roosevelt. And as a senior,

Robertson scored 39 points in a 79-56 championship victory against Lafayette Jeff, capping a 31-0 season.

Robertson, who averaged 28 points as a senior and 24 during his varsity career, was selected 1956's Mr. Basketball before enjoying splendid careers at the University of Cincinnati and then in the NBA with the then-Cincinnati Royals and the Milwaukee Bucks.

While most recognize Robertson as a prolific high school scorer—indeed he was—Crowe often told friends that most people overlooked how well the Big O played at the defensive end.

Usually assigned to an opponent's best scorer, Robertson embraced those challenges, and only once in his high school career did the Big O ever foul out of a game.

After the Tigers dropped a one-point decision at Connersville during the 1954-55 regular season, they never lost again with the Big O in the lineup.

Robertson led Crispus Attucks to victories in the final 45 high school games he played.

Crowe coached many excellent players at Crispus Attucks but said Robertson's attention to detail and passion for practice clearly establishes him as one of the top five talents ever to play the game in the Hoosier State.

For many, Robertson is Indiana's greatest of all time.

The Rocket Launches

The single blonde curl that fell in the middle of Rick Mount's forehead was distinctive. But it paled in comparison to the distinctive jump shot that made Lebanon

High School's prolific scorer the talk of the state during the mid-1960s.

To this day, only four Indiana high school school-boys—Bedford's Damon Bailey, Lewisville's Marion Pierce, Fort Wayne Bishop Luers' Deshaun Thomas, and Union/Dugger's Brody Boyd—scored more than Mount's 2,595 career points, compiled during four varsity seasons with the Tigers.

Indiana's 1966 Mr. Basketball—Mount averaged 33.1 points a game as a Lebanon senior—went on to Purdue, where he earned All-American honors in leading the Boilermakers to a second-place NCAA tournament finish in 1969, losing to John Wooden-coached UCLA in the title game.

But long before he became a Boilermaker, Mount, the son of former Lebanon standout Pete Mount, developed his long-range shooting skills the old-fashioned way—he earned it.

"When I was a kid, my dad cut a hole in the bottom of an old Planter's Peanuts can and instructed me to use a tennis ball to shoot at it," said Mount, who continues to stage form-shooting clinics for kids each summer.

"I didn't realize it at the time, but by shooting a tennis ball at that can, I developed great strength in my wrists. Most long-range shooters have very strong wrists."

In junior high school, Mount's scoring attracted large crowds to the Lebanon gym. This Boone County commu-nity located 30 miles north of Indianapolis knew it had something special.

Ever the perfectionist, Mount honed his shooting touch at Lebanon's City Park. He worked as a lifeguard at the swimming pool. During breaks, Mount snatched his basketball and raced to the park's outdoor basketball courts.

Rick Mount was the first high school athlete featured on Sports Illustrated*'s cover (Robert Huntzinger/Sports Illustrated)*

"I didn't have a lot of time during breaks, so I would ask a little kid to come and rebound for me," Mount said. "I would buy an ice cream cone for the kid who would retrieve the ball and pass it back to me. I had lots of takers on that offer."

Mount, who grew into a strong, 6-foot-4 shooting guard, earned a starting berth as a Lebanon High School freshman for coach Jim Rosenstihl. Those fans who didn't arrive at the gym during the junior varsity game often did not get a seat for the varsity contest.

Before Mount's senior season at Lebanon, he became the first high school basketball player ever featured on the cover of *Sports Illustrated*.

During that 1965-66 season, Mount led Lebanon into the Lafayette semistate's championship game—one victory from a coveted Final Four berth. But when Mount developed leg cramps during the second half, East Chicago Washington hung on for a close victory.

Mount scored a single-game-high 57 points during the 1965-66 season and was offered Division I scholarships from many schools.

Former Purdue assistant coach Bob King convinced Mount to sign with the Boilermakers after the standout shooter originally committed to Miami, Florida.

"Rick Mount—to this day—is the best pure shooter I've ever seen," King said. "He destroyed zone defenses, and if you tried to play him man-to-man, he would pull up and murder you with that quick release."

The Hick from French Lick

French Lick is a sleepy town, deep in Southern Indiana, where high school basketball players remain community icons.

There is no question about the identity of French Lick's favorite son—Larry Joe Bird, whose splendid careers at Indiana State University and with the NBA's Boston Celtics merely are sidebars to the fans of Springs Valley High School, where Bird first exhibited the skills that would make a millionaire of a young man whose parents barely made ends meet.

Gary Holland, who was Bird's junior varsity coach at Springs Valley, recalls that because Bird had neither a car nor spending money, the 6-foot-9 kid played basketball. Period.

Bird honed his perimeter shooting skills with hours and hours of form-shooting work. He could rebound with anybody at the high school level, and his passes were crisp and on the mark.

Bird's senior season—1973-74—at Springs Valley is one to remember. With a modest supporting cast, Bird averaged a school-record 30.6 points and an almost unheard-of 20 rebounds a game, helping his team post a 21-4 record.

Springs Valley won its sectional before dropping a tough 58-55 decision to Bedford-North Lawrence in the regional tournament. Still, Bird's senior season was more than enough to earn a slot on the coveted Indiana All-Star team, which annually plays Kentucky's best in a two-game June series.

During the regular season of his senior year, Bird scored a school-record 55 points against Corydon and took down 38 rebounds in a game against Bloomfield.

Bird certainly would have finished his high school career among Indiana's scoring leaders had he not broken an ankle in the first game of his sophomore season. Bird

Larry Bird of Springs Valley shoots over a Jasper defender.

returned for the final six games but really wasn't at 100 percent until his junior year.

While he never played in a state championship game, nor did he receive lots of media coverage at Springs Valley,

Bird certainly is among the greatest talents ever to come out of an Indiana high school.

After less than a month at Indiana University—Bird was overwhelmed by the size of the Bloomington campus—he quit college and returned to French Lick, where he worked on a garbage truck for almost a year.

Finally, the coaching staff at Indiana State University convinced Bird to try college again at the smaller Terre Haute-based campus. The rest is history. In 1979, Bird led ISU to the NCAA tournament's championship game, where Magic Johnson-led Michigan State edged Bird and the Sycamores.

Bird went to Boston, became an NBA legend, returned to Indiana to coach the NBA's Pacers and has continued to work for the franchise in multiple front office roles.

Not bad for a kid whose first job out of high school was collecting garbage. Only in Indiana, right?

A Weekend to Remember

Steve Alford has lived almost every Indiana schoolboy's basketball dream. He was selected the state's 1983 Mr. Basketball. He led Indiana University to the 1987 NCAA tournament championship. And he played several seasons in the NBA.

But the current head coach at UCLA fondly recalls a February weekend in 1983 as the best 48 hours a high school player could experience.

On a cold Friday night, Alford and his New Castle Trojans hosted North Central Conference rival Marion

*Steve Alford in the 1983 semistate contest
vs. Indianapolis Broad Ripple.*

in the 9,325-seat Chrysler Fieldhouse. Marion, led by University of Kentucky-bound James Blackmon, and New Castle were two of the favorites to win that year's state championship.

More than 10,000 tickets were sold, and 25 press credentials were issued to media members desiring to cover the game. Alford led his team to a 103-72 victory.

On Saturday night, Scott Hicks and Indianapolis Cathedral visited New Castle for another showdown of schoolboy heroes. Hicks, who was bound for Notre Dame, and his team attracted another standing-room-only crowd of 10,000.

Cathedral won by a single point on a last-second shot.

Alford, who averaged a state record-tying 37.2 points a game during the 1982-83 season, never will forget those two games.

"That was a neat weekend," Alford said. "I don't know of another high school player—and again, I've been very blessed—that accomplished what took place that weekend.

"There's not many high school players who can say they played in front of 20,000 people in a two-night period. That's what makes Indiana special. That's what made it a very humbling and honorable experience playing at New Castle with a gym capacity like that."

Less than a month later Alford scored a season-high 57 points in an Indianapolis semistate victory against Indianapolis Broad Ripple. Alford was 25 of 25 from the free throw line to go with 16 two-point field goals.

"People remember the points, but I took a lot of pride in free throw shooting," Alford said. "I'm more proud of the 25 of 25 from the line than I am of the actual point total."

The Hoosier Schoolboy Prototype

Good looks. Great skills. Golden-boy image.

If ever a child was born to play Indiana high school basketball, it was Damon Bailey, who became a Hoosier legend before he ever scored a single varsity point.

Bailey, a multifaceted 6-foot-3 guard, was raised in tiny Heltonville, Indiana, which is a part of the basketball-crazy Bedford-North Lawrence school district in southern Indiana.

As an eighth-grader, legendary college coach Bob Knight was spotted at one of Bailey's games, munching on a sack of popcorn while watching the player's every move.

When John Feinstein's *Season on the Brink* was published after Indiana University's 1985-86 season, the writer included a tale of Knight's drive back to Bloomington, during which the coach told others in the car that Bailey might be better than any guard on that IU team's roster.

Talk about pressure placed on an eighth-grader, especially one whose high school is only a short drive from IU's Bloomington campus.

But Knight—ever the excellent judge of talent—knew of what he spoke.

As a freshman, sophomore and senior, Bailey single-handedly led Bedford-North Lawrence to berths in the Indiana High School Athletic Association's one-class tournament's Final Four.

And in March 1990, Bailey capped a career that could only have been scripted in Hollywood, leading Bedford-North Lawrence to a 63-60 state-title game victory against Concord in front of more than 39,000 fans in

*Damon Bailey, the Indiana schoolboy legend,
became the state's career scoring leader.*

Indianapolis's RCA Dome—the first time the event was staged in that venue.

Bailey's clutch free throws in the closing seconds lifted the Stars to victory, capping a 29-2 season. Bailey, who played four seasons at IU for Knight, finished his four-year high school career with a state-record 3,134 points.

That record still stands.

In the moments after BNL's title game victory, Bailey raced into the RCA Dome stands to seek out his parents, whom he hugged with tears rolling down his cheeks.

Could Bailey's high school career have ended any other way? According to coach Dan Bush, Bailey was most deserving.

"Damon handled everything, the media, opponents, the hype, fans' expectations, as well as any kid ever could," Bush said.

Just how crazy were the people of Lawrence County about Bailey?

Try this one.

In order to ensure a ticket for the Seymour sectional tournament in which BNL competed, more than 500 Bedford-North Lawrence fans purchased regular-season season tickets for Seymour's 1990-91 campaign.

The kicker? BNL fans never used those season tickets. But when it came time for the sectional, it was as if Bedford-North Lawrence was the home team.

Damon Bailey created that passion for BNL basketball, carving a legend that will be discussed for generations to come.

Big Dog, Big Bite

So painfully shy. So magnificently talented.

Like many of his friends who grew up in the often rugged streets of Gary, Indiana, Glenn Robinson had a difficult time with trust. Robinson, however, trusted his basketball skills, which helped him secure a slot among Indiana's legends.

Robinson's home was a long three-pointer from the doors of Gary Roosevelt High School, where coach Ron Heflin became the adult male role model "Big Dog" needed.

"You could see the raw talent when he was an eighth-grader," Heflin recalled. "We just had to convince him how good he could be."

While Robinson isn't among Indiana's top 25 career scorers, his complete game, coupled with a terrific 1990-91 season during which he averaged 25 points a contest, places him on the short list of Hoosier State greats.

Gary Roosevelt finished Robinson's senior season with a 30-1 record and Indiana's then-single-class state championship.

In one of the state's most anticipated championship games, Robinson was a defensive demon, dominating the interior in Roosevelt's 51-32 victory against Indianapolis Brebeuf and Alan Henderson.

Robinson went on to star at Purdue, and Henderson played for rival Indiana. Each has enjoyed a solid career in the National Basketball Association. In 1994, the Milwaukee Bucks used the first selection in the amateur draft to select Robinson—the shy kid who blossomed on the basketball court.

Glenn Robinson led Gary Roosevelt to the 1991 state title.

"The thing most people don't realize about Glenn is that not only was he our most talented player, but during his second season at Purdue, he became our hardest worker," Purdue coach Gene Keady recalls.

"Once Glenn began to play defense as we asked, he became a complete player."

Robinson was selected Indiana's 1991 Mr. Basketball, joining a long list of Hoosier schoolboy greats who have earned the award. To this day, Robinson often returns to his hometown to stage youth basketball clinics, encouraging kids to stay in school.

"Some people misunderstood Glenn's shyness," Heflin said. "But Glenn Robinson always will be special to the people of Gary."

One of a Kind

Stephanie White's fondest childhood memories are too numerous to count, although playing basketball every Sunday afternoon with her father and his friends at the Seeger Memorial Gymnasium in Warren County is at the top of the list.

When told she played like a boy, Stephanie gladly accepted the compliment.

Those Sunday sessions were the beginning of a legend that—to this day—is among Indiana girls' basketball's most heartwarming stories.

White, who led the Purdue women's basketball team to the 1999 NCAA tournament championship, burst onto Indiana's high school scene as a Seeger freshman in 1991-92, when she averaged 19.4 points in helping the Lady Patriots compile a 21-3 record.

As a sophomore, White averaged 28.3 points—including a single-game high of 43—in a 23-1 campaign. Her junior year was better. White averaged 31.0 points a game, including a 56-point game, and Seeger won 25 of 27 games.

Entering her senior year, everyone associated with Seeger basketball knew White was on the verge of becoming Indiana's female career scoring leader.

In 1994-95, White began a pursuit of the 2,421 points scored by former North Judson standout Debbie Bolen, who completed her high school playing career in 1988.

As White closed in on Bolen's record, team and school officials realized White probably would break Bolen's record in a regular-season game scheduled to be played at

Stephanie White of Seeger was Indiana's 1995 Miss
Basketball.

Wabash River Conference foe Turkey Run, whose gym's seating capacity is less than 2,000.

With Turkey Run's blessing, the game site was switched to nearby Fountain Central, whose gymnasium is 1,300 seats larger than Turkey Run's facility.

On the night White shattered Bolen's mark, a standing-room-only gathering estimated at 3,000 watched White make history while leading the Lady Patriots to an easy victory.

While White's dream of playing in the state finals was cut short by Lake Central in the Lafayette semistate, the terrific player from West Lebanon, Indiana finished her senior season averaging 36.9 points with a single-game best of 66.

In four varsity seasons, White scored a state record 2,869 points, averaging 28.9 points a game. Of the 99 games White played at Seeger, the Patriots won 92.

Only in the semistate were opponents able to get the best of White-led teams; Valparaiso, Gary West and Lake Central (twice) ended White's attempt to lead tiny Seeger to the Final Four.

Still, her personality, ability and knack for rising to the occasion make White the most popular high school girl in Indiana basketball history.

After the 1994-95 season, White was selected Indiana's Miss Basketball and also picked National Player of the Year by almost every publication.

CHAPTER 2

EARLY PLAYERS AND COACHES

Warm and "Fuzzy" in Franklin

Winning back-to-back Indiana high school boys' basketball state championships is difficult enough, but three in a row? That's an extraordinary milestone.

Franklin had an "extraordinary" player—Robert "Fuzzy" Vandivier—during the 1920, 1921 and 1922 state tournaments, when it became the first and one of only two Indiana high schools to collect three consecutive state titles.

Marion—in 1985, 1986 and 1987—was the only other back-to-back-to-back champ until Indianapolis Lawrence North High School did so in 2004, 2005 and 2006.

Vandivier, who died in 1983 at the age of 79, led Franklin to the then-16-team state finals in 1919, when he was a freshman. Franklin was eliminated in the opening round by Crawfordsville. Franklin would not lose another

Fuzzy Vandivier (as a player above and as coach below)
led Franklin to three state crowns.

tournament game as long as Vandivier was a high school student.

During Vandivier's sophomore, junior and senior seasons, Franklin won 89 of 98 games, including a 29-1 mark when he was a 10th-grader.

He finished four years of varsity play with 1,540 points. Not until 1950—28 years after Vandivier's final high school game—did another Indiana prep player score as many as 1,500 points during his career.

Vandivier made Franklin coach Ernest "Griz" Wagner a legend in the Johnson County community, just a few miles south of the Greater Indianapolis area.

After Vandivier scored 10 and 17 points, respectively, in state tourney semifinal and final game victories against Anderson and Lafayette Jeff, respectively, the citizens of Franklin took up a collection to reward Wagner.

Believe it or not, he was presented with $1,000, which was considered a fortune in 1920.

Not to be outdone, Vandivier and Franklin were at it again in 1921, defeating the same teams—Lafayette Jeff and Anderson—but in a different order during the state finals' semifinal and title games.

Vandivier scored nine points in a 17-12 victory against Lafayette Jeff, then 13 in the 35-22 championship game victory against Anderson.

As a senior, Vandivier paced Franklin to a 31-4 record, including Final Four victories against Bloomington (33-17) and Terre Haute Garfield (26-15). In his final two high school games, Vandivier contributed 13 and 12 points, respectively.

Vandivier went on to coach his alma mater in the 1930s, just missing a title in 1939 when Franklin lost to Frankfort in the state championship game.

In 1962, Vandivier was among the first class inducted into Indiana's Basketball Hall of Fame. In 1975, he was inducted into the Naismith Hall of Fame in Springfield, Massachusetts.

"Put Him in the Game"

As an impressionable middle school student growing up in southern Indiana as our nation celebrated its victory in World World II, Gene Cato spent most Friday nights from November through March glued to the family's radio, straining to hear play-by-play of mighty Evansville Central's basketball games.

Cato imagined sinking a game-winning shot for Central and playing deep into Indiana's fabled state tournament.

He honed his ball-handling and shooting skills under the watchful eye of his father, Alva, the high school coach at tiny Lynville in Warrick County, an hour's drive from the bright lights of Evansville.

By the 1946-47 high school season, Gene Cato was a talented sophomore guard whose skills surpassed most junior and senior members of Alva Cato's team. But in small-town Indiana, there couldn't be a hint of father/coach favoritism.

Sophomore Gene Cato was doing more sitting than playing, and Lynville was a basketball team spinning its wheels.

"It was my sophomore year, and I think everyone in the community knew that I probably should be starting," said Gene Cato, the IHSAA's commissioner during most of the 1980s and '90s after a stellar career as a teacher, coach and administrator at Zionsville High School. "But if you knew my father, the last person that he was going to give a break to was his son.

"He told me, 'I'm not going to start you, Gene. You're good enough to start, but until these fans come to me and tell me that I should be playing you, you're not going to start.' I remember telling him, 'Dad, they may never do that.'"

Fortunately for Lynville, Gene Cato and Alva Cato, the team's loyal fans voiced their desire at the next game. "We want Gene, we want Gene," the Lynville fans chanted.

Gene Cato became a starter, and Lynville became a small-school power. Gene Cato led Warrick County in scoring during the 1947-48 season, after which his father was offered the head coaching position at Oakland City High School in nearby Gibson County.

In 1948-49, Gene Cato—then an Oakland City High School senior—led Gibson County in scoring. To this day, Gene Cato remains one of the few Indiana high school players ever to lead two different counties in scoring in back-to-back seasons.

"My father was a very wise man," Gene Cato said. "I didn't know it at the time, but my dad was taking all the pressure off my back. He placed me in a position to be successful."

Cato's grandson, Michael Lewis, became one of southern Indiana's most prolific scorers at Jasper High School, earning a scholarship to Indiana University, where he played for the legendary Bob Knight.

Gene Cato passed away in 2008 at age 77.

The King of Loogootee

The numbers are staggering. The story is more improbable than the staggering numbers. But ornery and colorful Jack Butcher wouldn't have it any other way.

Loogootee's former boys' basketball coach is the king of his domain and the Hoosier State's coaching victory list. To be exact, Butcher won 806 varsity games—all at his beloved Loogootee. No Indiana high school basketball coach has more.

This splendid story of home and one man's loyalty to it begins in 1951, when Jack Butcher graduated from Loogootee High School in a community of 2,741 in southern Indiana.

Butcher joined the military, served his country during the Korean War, then returned to civilian life, where a basketball scholarship from Memphis State University was waiting for him.

The good-shooting guard led the Tigers to the 1956 NCAA tournament, where he earned All-Regional honors. In 1957, he helped Memphis State to a second-place finish in the National Invitation Tournament in New York City.

The Boston Celtics thought so much of Butcher's ability that they selected him in the NBA draft. Butcher was flattered, but he longed for the simple life of Loogootee and was eager to begin a teaching and coaching career.

In 1957, Butcher was offered a teaching position that would include the assignment as assistant basketball coach at his beloved Loogootee.

On the first day of practice, Butcher walked into the locker room, where he was greeted by the head coach. The next words Butcher heard were mind-boggling.

*Jack Butcher became a coaching legend
in his hometown of Loogootee.*

The head coach tossed the keys to the locker room in Butcher's direction and said, "Here you go, kid, you're on your own."

For the next 45 years, one man coached varsity basketball at Loogootee—favorite son Jack Butcher. While the Lions posted a sub-.500 record in Butcher's first season, that happened only once more in his final 44 years.

He guided Loogootee to the single-class Final Four in 1970 and again in 1975.

His 1970 team was beaten 71-62 by Carmel in the semifinals, and his 1975 team advanced to the state championship game before losing to Marion, 58-46.

Butcher came oh so very close to a state crown in the multiple-class tournament setting in 2001. Loogootee was beaten in overtime by eventual Class A state champion Attica in the Greencastle semistate title game. Attica then went on to beat Blue River in the championship game in Conseco Fieldhouse.

In winning those 806 games, Butcher exhibited his coaching flexibility.

But Butcher's philosophy changed in the mid-1970s, when he taught his teams to control the tempo with keen shot selection, often winning games by scores of 32-30 or 40-35.

"The game is about finding the best possible shot," Butcher told his players and colleagues.

He also strongly believed that games often were won—or lost—before either team attempted the first shot. Butcher was a stickler for preparation, imploring his players to go beyond the 100-percent effort level during practices.

Butcher stressed fundamentals, but above all, he stressed selflessness. He wanted his players to lose themselves to the team and accept any role to which they were assigned.

Jack Butcher never won an Indiana state championship, but no coach in this basketball-crazy state ever won more games than Loogootee's Legend.

The Hurricane

Lewisville, Indiana, is a tiny dot in Rand McNally's atlas, a few miles south of the New Castle-based Indiana Basketball Hall of Fame.

When lanky Marion Pierce enrolled as a Lewisville High School freshman in the fall of 1957, four-grade enrollment was 80—give or take a student.

Little did anyone know that during the next four Indiana high school basketball seasons, the quiet, 6-foot-5 kid with a passion for jump shots and motorbikes would establish a career scoring record that would last for 29 years, until 1991 Mr. Basketball Damon Bailey from Bedford-North Lawrence shattered it.

Pierce's father, G.W. Pierce, supported nine children with his Henry County-based wreckyard/junkyard. While each of the family's seven sons were expected to help with the business, G.W. also encouraged his boys to play basketball.

While the others were fine players in their own right at Lewisville—now part of the consolidation known as Tri-High—Marion Pierce was the chosen one.

In 1957-58, Pierce averaged 20.2 points. As a sophomore, he averaged a state-best 34.6, including a career-best 64 against Union Township. As a high school junior, the center/power forward averaged 36.4, again leading the state.

Like most Indiana schoolboy legends, Pierce saved his best for last—in more ways than one.

In 1960-61, he averaged a state-leading 38.2 points, helping Lewisville win the school's first sectional championship since 1945.

In the New Castle sectional semifinals, Pierce scored 43 points in a thrilling 72-70, double-overtime victory against Middletown, setting up a grudge match against North Central Conference power New Castle in that night championship game.

Lady luck may have smiled on Pierce and the Lewisville Bears in the moments after their victory against Middletown.

With snow blanketing all of Henry County, a power line near the New Castle Chrysler Fieldhouse fell, knocking out electricity in the 9,300-seat venue.

Sectional tournament and Indiana High School Athletic Association officials—acting on behalf of the safety of players, students and fans—postponed the New Castle sectional title game until Monday evening.

Short on depth compared to New Castle, the extra rest was just what Pierce and the Bears needed. Only 48 hours after the giant snowstorm, Pierce overcame second-quarter foul trouble, scored 27 points and led Lewisville to a 56-49 sectional title game victory against New Castle.

One week later, Pierce's 25 points weren't enough in a 50-41 New Castle regional loss to Muncie Central, whose eight state championships are more than any other Indiana high school boys basketball program.

*Marion Pierce passes the state scoring torch to Damon
Bailey.*

Pierce finished his four-year high school career with 3,019 points.

Twenty-nine seasons later, Bailey capped his four-year high school career with 3,134 points.

During the summer of 1961, Pierce was selected to the Indiana High School All-Star team that annually battles Kentucky.

Pierce played one season of junior college ball, averaging 32 points a game for Lindsey Wilson Junior College in Kentucky, but didn't enjoy school.

Shunning scholarship offers from Louisiana State, Miami, Florida, and Houston, Pierce decided to stay home in Lewisville, joining his father's business on a full-time basis.

Pierce, however, continued to play recreational-league basketball in the New Castle/Richmond area in eastern Indiana for the next 20 years. He also drove motorbikes competitively, carving quite a Midwestwide niche for himself.

But those who saw the player known as the "Henry County Hurricane" shoot a basketball know that while he was reared and educated in small-town Indiana, his skills were as good as his big-school counterparts, and his scoring ability was second to none for 29 years.

Kokomo's Goose Wins a Title

Indiana's rich basketball history includes many colorful characters. None, however, experienced more triumph and disaster than the late, great, colorful Jim "Goose"

Ligon, who in 1961 led Kokomo to its only boys' basketball state championship.

At 6-foot-7 and 210 pounds, Ligon possessed the interior skills of a seven-footer. At the same time, he could handle the ball, shoot with great accuracy and find the open man with a pinpoint pass.

Ligon was a junior when the Wildkats coasted into the 1961 Final Four with a 26-1 record, including a 10-game winning streak.

During an afternoon semifinal game against Logansport, Ligon had 29 points and 14 rebounds, leading Kokomo to an easy 87-66 victory.

In a classic state championship game performance, Ligon amassed 19 points and 24 rebounds before fouling out in overtime against Indianapolis Manual, which was led by twins Tom and Dick Van Arsdale.

Dick Van Arsdale tied the game at 66 with 26 seconds remaining. Kokomo called a timeout with 19 seconds to go, setting up a play for forward Ron Hughes.

Hughes was fouled with three seconds to play. He sank both free throws, giving Kokomo its 68-66 overtime victory.

While Hughes finished with a team-best 20 points, there was no question as to the best player on the floor that day. Against two top-flight opponents, Ligon compiled 48 points and 42 rebounds.

As a senior, Ligon's numbers were better. He averaged 29.9 points, including a single-game high of 53. Kokomo returned to the Final Four, but its bid for back-to-back state crowns was halted when East Chicago Washington overcame Ligon's 25 points and beat the Wildkats, 74-73, in the state semifinals.

Ligon finished his high school career with exactly 1,900 points, which to this day is a Howard County record.

While Ligon was the ultimate standout on a basketball court, trouble often followed him. In 1963, he was convicted of a crime and spent three and a half years in a state correctional facility.

After his release in 1967, Ligon returned to the game he loved, playing the next seven seasons in the American Basketball Association, primarily with the Kentucky Colonels.

Ligon averaged 12.8 points and 10.9 rebounds in his seven ABA seasons. But he often was plagued by drug and alcohol problems and played his last professional game in 1975.

From that time until his death in April 2004, Ligon's life was on a constant roller coaster. He made time to coach kids' basketball in Louisville, but he also found himself abusing alcohol and drugs, which led to heart problems and eventually a mild stroke.

Ligon returned to Kokomo in the fall of 2003 to be inducted into the Howard County Hall of Fame—an honor that truly touched him. He told friends how happy he was to be recognized after so many years.

Only seven months later, Ligon died at the Hospice of Louisville.

Fred Fleetwood, a 1962 Southport graduate who roomed with Ligon during the Indiana-Kentucky All-Star series, thoroughly enjoyed being around Ligon and having the opportunity to play alongside him.

"Goose was so misunderstood," Fleetwood said. "The Goose loved people, and he loved basketball. He truly was

Goose Ligon (No. 22) led Kokomo to the 1961 state title.

a great guy. But Goose was afraid ... afraid of many things. When we roomed together, he would lock the door and push a chair up against it.

"When I asked him why, he said it was because he didn't want anyone to bother him. He experienced some sad things, but I can tell you that Goose Ligon was a nice man and a hell of a player."

In Evansville, It's a Small World

Just before World War II, and then during it, those in Evansville who love their basketball had many opportunities to take their minds off the horrors that were occurring in Europe and in the South Pacific.

In 1939, Evansville Bosse made its way to the IHSAA's Final Four led by a handsome, hot-shooting forward named Jim Myers.

While Myers's 13 points in the semifinal game against eventual champion Frankfort weren't enough, Myers's academics, citizenship and athletic skills were recognized when he received the Gimbel Medal, presented by the IHSAA for the outstanding Final Four student/athlete.

Then, in 1944 and again in 1945, Julius "Bud" Ritter led the Bulldogs to back-to-back state titles. In the 1944 state finals, Ritter scored 13 points in a 41-38 victory against LaPorte and then seven in a 39-35 title game victory against Kokomo.

In 1945, Ritter helped Bosse to a 25-2 mark and a second consecutive state crown. He had six points in a 37-35 victory against Indianapolis Broad Ripple and 14 in a 46-36 title game victory against South Bend Riley.

It certainly was a small world 17 years later, when Myers—then coach of his alma mater—and Ritter—highly successful coach at unbeaten Madison—found themselves on opposite benches for a thrilling Final Four semifinal battle at Hinkle Fieldhouse in Indianapolis.

Myers's Bosse team got 19 points from forward Gene Lockyear and 17 from forward Gary Grieger in a 79-75 victory against Madison and Ritter.

In the state championship game, Myers led Bosse to an 84-81 triumph against East Chicago Washington.

Ironically, Myers failed to secure a state title as a player but earned one as a coach. Ritter earned two state titles as a player but never got one as a coach, denied the 1962 championship by his alma mater.

The Chubby Kid Shines

With the possible exception of Reggie Miller, it would be difficult to challenge Billy Keller as the most popular Indiana Pacer of all time.

But during the early 1960s, Keller never could have imagined playing professional basketball. Keller was just hoping to hone his skills enough to earn a varsity spot on the Indianapolis Washington High School roster.

As a seventh-grader, Keller began tagging along with an older brother and his friends when they would travel to Meadowood Park to play basketball on the outdoor courts.

Keller disliked being called "tubby" and "meatballs" by the older kids, but he was determined to be the best basketball player a short, overweight kid could be. He played some and watched a lot.

But Billy Keller was smart and understood the work ethic needed to play varsity basketball. Those older boys who played at Meadowood included some of Indianapolis's best.

In 1962 and 1963, Keller shot the ball twice as many times as most kids his age. Practice, he learned, would make him as close to perfect as a 5-foot-10 kid could be.

*Bill Keller (left in white) in the 1965 state championship
game.*

He slimmed down, losing some of the baby fat and replacing it with muscle from countless hours playing ball.

When the 1964-65 season began, Washington senior guard Billy Keller was ready to show the state that he could play this game. And win.

Keller became the undisputed leader of a Washington Continentals team that would win 29 of 31 games, including a 64-57 victory against Fort Wayne North in the state championship game, during which Keller scored 25 points.

In the Final Four semifinal victory against Princeton, Keller scored 22 of his team's 88 in an 88-76 triumph.

Keller was selected Indiana's Mr. Basketball and accepted a basketball scholarship to Purdue, where he played for George King.

In 1968-69, Keller and 1966 Mr. Basketball Rick Mount from Lebanon led Purdue to the NCAA tournament's championship game in which the Boilermakers were beaten by UCLA, coached by former Indiana high school and Purdue great John Wooden.

Keller remains one of Purdue's career leading scorers and helped the Indiana Pacers win an American Basketball Association championship.

Not bad for a chubby kid.

It's All an Act

In 1983, Mike Warren—standout performer in the NBC hit series *Hill Street Blues*—was nominated for an

Emmy, the highest honor bestowed by the television industry.

In 1963, Mike Warren—standout performer for the South Bend Central basketball team—led the Bears to within one victory of Indiana's coveted state championship.

Yes, it's the same Mike Warren.

Warren, a slick guard, was a two-time All-State selection who scored 43 points in an Elkhart regional victory on his way to playing in the 1963 state finals.

Once on center stage at Hinkle Fieldhouse, Warren scored nine points and handed out several assists in South Bend Central's 72-45 semifinal victory against Terre Haute Garfield.

In the championship game, Warren poured in 11 field goals for a game-high 22 points, but Muncie Central's balance was too much for South Bend Central, and the Bearcats hung on for a 65-61 thriller.

Upon graduation from South Bend Central, Warren accepted former Hoosier legend John Wooden's basketball scholarship offer to attend UCLA.

Playing with Lew Alcindor—now Kareem-Abdul Jabbar—Warren was a three-year Bruins starter and a two-time captain, helping UCLA win NCAA tournament championships in 1967 and again in 1968.

While most of America knows Warren as an accomplished dramatic actor, old-timers in South Bend say he was one of the most intelligent, good-shooting guards the city ever has produced.

In 1992, Warren was selected to the Indiana Basketball Hall of Fame, which is based in New Castle.

Evansville North's Music Man

For most of two decades, Saturday afternoon and evening Big Ten Conference men's basketball telecasts have featured a familiar face and voice to those who call Indiana—specifically Evansville or West Lafayette—home.

Former Evansville North High School and Purdue University standout basketball player Bob Ford is among the Big Ten's most experienced color analysts.

Mackey Arena. The Jack Breslin Center. Carver-Hawkeye Arena. You name the Big Ten venue, and Ford has called many games there.

However, long before he began a career in broadcasting, Ford did two things extremely well—play basketball and sing.

While a student at Purdue from the fall of 1968 through the spring of 1972, Bob Ford was a member of the prestigious Purdue Glee Club—a singing group that travels the world giving performances.

Ford also was a splendid college basketball player, helping support high-scoring Rick Mount during Mount's senior season of 1969-70.

But Ford burst onto the basketball scene during Evansville North's memorable 1966-67 state championship season, when, as a junior on a senior-dominated team, he carried the Huskies to the school's first boys' basketball state championship.

Evansville North lost regular-season games to Evansville Bosse and Evansville Harrison, entering the always-difficult Evansville sectional with an 18-2 mark. Because the Huskies' schedule included teams only from southwestern Indiana, the other 75 percent of the state knew little—if anything—about the 6-foot-7 Ford and Co.

North survived a four-point scare from Evansville Reitz in the sectional opener, then coasted into the Evansville semistate's championship game, where an extremely talented and favored Terre Haute Garfield team was waiting.

With Ford doing plenty of damage inside, Evansville North clipped Terre Haute Garfield 59-58, earning a trip to the Final Four in Indianapolis.

Given his first statewide audience, Ford opened many eyes, scoring 35 points in Evansville North's 66-56 semifinal victory against North Central Conference power New Castle.

In the state championship game, Ford was at it again, pouring in 27 points in the Huskies' 60-58 victory against Lafayette Jeff, denying legendary coach Marion Crawley what would have been a fifth state championship. Crawley retired after the 1966-67 season.

Ford enjoyed an excellent senior season, but with his supporting cast from 1967 gone, the Huskies failed to get back to Indianapolis and the Final Four.

He was, however, selected to play for the Indiana All-Stars in their annual two-game June showdown with the best high school players from Kentucky.

The Evansville North big man accepted coach George King's scholarship offer to play basketball at Purdue, ending his Boilermaker career with 1,244 points.

Ford averaged 19.8 points a game as a junior and 19.6 as a senior. He also shot 50.3 percent from the field during his Purdue career.

After a brief professional playing career with the American Basketball Association's Memphis Tams, Ford

*Bob Ford was a star at Purdue after leading
Evansville North to the 1967 state title.*

entered the media industry, serving for many years as station manager at WLFI-TV in Lafayette before becoming involved in an advertising agency.

Ford grins when asked if he still can carry a tune, nodding affirmatively while noting that his voice is better used today in the basketball broadcasting industry.

The singing big man's son, Andrew, followed in his father's footsteps, playing basketball at Purdue after a four-year varsity career at West Lafayette High School.

The Greenfield Gunner

One of Indiana's favorite early morning coffee shop topics of discussion is determining the finest perimeter shooter this state ever has produced.

Many names are tossed into the conversation arena. Lebanon's Rick Mount. New Castle's Steve Alford. Peru's Kyle Macy. Plymouth's Scott Skiles. Valparaiso's Bryce Drew. Kokomo's Jimmy Rayl. Carmel's Billy Shepherd.

Actually, the list goes on and on, although those in the 45-and-over club usually give Mount the nod.

However, those who live in or near Hancock County, just a long three-pointer from Indianapolis's east side, will tell you that Greenfield's Mike Edwards—affectionately known as "The Greenfield Gunner"—could shoot with any player on any given day.

While Edwards's teams never received the statewide publicity tossed at traditional powers Marion, Muncie Central or Indianapolis Pike, the 6-foot-4 guard possessed a silky-smooth touch.

To this day, Edwards's 2,343 career points rank seventh in Indiana high school basketball history. Damon Bailey, the former Bedford-North Lawrence and Indiana University star, is No. 1 with 3,134 points.

But what makes Edwards such a popular Hoosier legend is how well he played in his final two high school seasons, when every coach on Greenfield's schedule devised a defensive set with one purpose and one purpose only—stop Edwards.

Trouble was, nothing stopped Edwards during his junior and senior seasons.

In 1967-68, Edwards stepped out of a shadow and into the spotlight, averaging an astounding 34.4 points as a Greenfield junior.

Then, in 1968-69, Edwards took it up another notch, pouring in 36.4 points a game. In 25 games, Edwards scored 910 points, including a school single-game-record 57 points.

Edwards was selected to a terrific Indiana All-Star team that included Mr. Basketball George McGinnis. Edwards went on to play three seasons of varsity basketball at the University of Tennessee, where he was the Southeastern Conference Player of the Year in 1972.

He finished his collegiate career with 1,343 points and All-SEC honors in 1972 and again in 1973. Edwards played professionally in Mexico before returning to the United States, where he coached high school basketball in Tennessee. Edwards then joined the collegiate coaching fraternity, working at several small colleges.

Edwards's long-range shooting skills often make Hancock County fans speculate as to how many points he would have scored in 1968 and 1969 had the three-point line been in effect at that period in basketball history.

But three-pointer or no three-pointer, "The Greenfield Gunner" remains one of Indiana's legendary shooters in a state known for its ability to produce those who know how to put the ball in the basket.

Big Mac Attacks

Those who watched George McGinnis play professionally for the Indiana Pacers and the Philadelphia 76ers were impressed with the 6-foot-8 power player's ability to attack the basket one minute, then pull up and sink a perimeter shot the next time down the floor.

Those were skills McGinnis developed at Indianapolis Washington High School, where during the 1968-69 season, he and 6-foot-9 Steve Downing formed what probably is the finest big-man combo in Indiana high school basketball history.

McGinnis and Downing, who were college teammates at Indiana University, led the 1969 Washington Continentals to a perfect 31-0 season and their school's second state championship in four years.

Recruited by several major colleges to play tight end, McGinnis sealed his future as a basketball player during a Final Four for the ages.

Indianapolis Washington, Marion and Vincennes each entered the Final Four unbeaten, and Gary Tolleston came to Indianapolis with but a single loss.

*George McGinnis was the star of
Indianapolis Washington's 1969 state champs.*

Marion appeared to have Indianapolis Washington beaten during the first afternoon semifinal, but Downing sank a shot with 20 seconds remaining, then blocked Marion's last-gasp attempt at the other end, with McGinnis hauling down the rebound.

McGinnis scored 27 points in the victory against Marion.

In the state championship game, McGinnis put on a show, scoring 35 points in a 79-76 victory against Gary Tolleston.

Including Indianapolis semistate victories against Silver Creek and Jac-Cen-Del, McGinnis scored 148 points in his team's final four games—an average of 37 points.

In recent years, McGinnis often has deflected credit for Indianapolis Washington's unbeaten 1969 season, saying that without Downing, the Continentals likely would have fallen short in their quest.

But along with Oscar Robertson, who led Indianapolis Crispus Attucks to the 1955 and 1956 state championships, a strong case can be built that McGinnis is one of the two finest players ever to come out of Indiana's largest city.

A Home Away from Home

A venue such as New Castle's 9,325-seat Chrysler Fieldhouse is an intimidating place for most high school basketball players, especially those who do not play for the hometown Trojans.

But Rick Peckinpaugh, who played for Sulphur Springs in 1966-67 and then for the consolidation known as Shenandoah during his final three high school seasons, was right at home in the state's largest on-site high school gymnasium, where former NBA players Kent Benson and Steve Alford earned "Hoosier Hysteria" legends status.

"Back then, the big school/small school thing was everywhere in the sectionals," Peckinpaugh said. "Nobody ever beat the big schools."

As a Shenandoah senior, Peckinpaugh's team was 20-1 as it prepared to play New Castle in the 1970 New Castle sectional semifinals.

While the Trojans built a halftime lead against Shenandoah, Peckinpaugh remained confident. He walked by coach Ray Pavy—bound to a wheelchair after being paralyzed in an automobile accident in the early 1960s—and said, "Don't worry, Coach, we've got this one."

Sure enough, Peckinpaugh led a second-half charge, and Shenandoah stunned big-school power New Castle by 10 points. In the sectional final, Shenandoah defeated Knightstown by six. Peckinpaugh and his teammates delivered the school's first sectional title in its third year of existence.

Benson, who went on to star at Indiana University and then with the NBA's Detroit Pistons, was New Castle's freshman center in 1969-70. Peckinpaugh jumped center against the 6-foot-11 Benson in Shenandoah's victory against the Trojans.

The significance of Shenandoah's 1970 victory was put in perspective in 1971, when Benson led New Castle to the Final Four.

After beating New Castle and Knightstown for the 1970 New Castle sectional crown, Shenandoah—a consolidation of Middletown, Sulphur Springs and Cadiz—rolled into the New Castle regional with a 22-1 record.

In the first regional semifinal game, Shenandoah eased past Union, earning a spot in the title game against sixth-ranked Muncie Central, which had beaten Richmond in the morning session.

Peckinpaugh started quickly, and this team, which included four starters who averaged in double figures, found itself with an 18-point lead with 3:41 remaining in the third quarter.

But Peckinpaugh, who averaged 18 points a game during his senior season, picked up three fouls during the next 4:41, fouling out with seven minutes to play. He scored 19 points that night.

Muncie Central was energized by Peckinpaugh's fifth foul, turning an 18-point deficit into a 17-point victory—a 35-point swing in the game's final 11:41.

It wasn't the desired ending, but Peckinpaugh proved he was a player with whom to be reckoned in New Castle's enormous high school gym.

As a high school junior, Peckinpaugh hit a shot at the buzzer to beat Knightstown after having missed a potential game winner with 12 seconds to go.

"I went from the goat to the hero in about two seconds," Peckinpaugh said.

His first New Castle sectional "hero status" was earned in 1967, when, as a freshman in the final year Sulphur Springs was a high school, Peckinpaugh scored 23 points in a double-overtime victory against Blue River Valley.

"I was just out there," Peckinpaugh said. "I didn't know what I was doing. I made second-team All-Sectional as a freshman."

Peckinpaugh went on to play at Indiana State University, then coached at Muncie Central as an assistant in 1978 and 1979, when the Bearcats won back-to-back state championships.

He was the head coach for several seasons at Avon before moving onto McCutcheon, where his 1994 team reached the Lafayette semistate with his son, Chad, as the team's standout guard and leading scorer.

To this day, Rick Peckinpaugh loves reliving his four New Castle sectional experiences.

"That was a fantastic place to walk in and play," Peckinpaugh said. "At that time, the place would be packed. All the little schools hadn't consolidated yet.

"Watching my son play in the Lafayette sectional, the Lafayette regional and then the Lafayette semi-state in Purdue's Mackey Arena tops everything, but as a player, my top thrill was beating New Castle in their fieldhouse in the sectional. It couldn't be any better than that for a high school player."

While Peckinpaugh had lots of natural ability, he credits Pavy, who was a star at New Castle 10 years before coaching at Shenandoah, for helping him believe he could perform well in front of a such a large crowd in such an intimidating building.

"When you talk about playing for Shenandoah, you have to talk about playing for Ray Pavy," Peckinpaugh said. "It was very inspirational seeing this guy out there doing what he was doing in life when he was in a wheel-chair. What a great man."

A Shot for Solidarity

Jeff Mathew is a friendly, likeable man who plays and teaches golf as well as any Indiana-based club professional.

But during the 1971-72 Indiana high school basketball season, the quick, good-shooting guard teamed with fellow Wolcott resident Len Fulkerson to give Tri-County High School a lethal one-two punch in its first season as a consolidation.

Problem was, the residents of this White County-based school—of the towns of Remington and Wolcott—were about as happy as Purdue and Indiana fans would be if it was announced the schools' athletic programs were merging to form a single unit.

Moods went from bad to worse when the Cavaliers lost their first two games. Suddenly, coach Rod Nesius' team began to click, thanks in large part to Mathew and Fulkerson.

Including a Friday night victory against North Newton in early January, Tri-County won 11 in a row, setting the stage for the Cavaliers' test against big school Harrison (1,000 students in 1971-72) on the Saturday night after beating North Newton.

However, this team, which would finish 19-4, learned Saturday morning that it had a problem. Four varsity team members celebrated the North Newton victory a bit too much and missed Coach Nesius' curfew, earning one-game suspensions.

While star players Mathew and Fulkerson were not involved in the Friday night festivities, Tri-County would have only seven varsity players in uniform to take on Harrison.

Mathew, now in his mid-60s, still believes to this day that something magical was in the air that night in the old Wolcott gym, which served as Tri-County's home until the new school building and gym were completed in time for the 1972-73 school year.

As if a script had been handed down from Hollywood, Tri-County's Mathew hit the game-winning shot in an emotion-packed 69-67 victory against Harrison.

"Harrison was a big game for us, because it was a chance to play a big school," Mathew said. "As juniors at Wolcott, we had gotten annihilated playing at Harrison. This was our opportunity, but we thought it had fallen by the wayside with the one-game suspensions.

"Before the game, I honestly don't think Coach Nesius thought we could beat Harrison with only seven guys. As we were about to leave the locker room, he said, 'You guys really think you are going to beat them?' We said, 'Yes, we do.'"

During warmups, Tri-County almost exhausted itself during two-line layups. Players had to sprint to form the other side of the line.

Harrison raced to an early lead and maintained it through the third quarter. However, Tri-County's first basketball team specialized in comebacks and began another one early in the fourth period after trailing 20-13, 34-29 and 53-49 at the first three breaks.

"We hadn't played too well, which probably was a credit to Harrison," Mathew said. "Then, we kind of caught up at the end, got the ball back and called a timeout with only a few seconds remaining."

During the timeout, Coach Nesius called play "No. 5," an inbounds pass designed to get the ball into Mathew's hands.

"Somehow, when I got the ball, I was a little farther out than I hoped to be," Mathew said. "It was designed for a 15-foot shot, but I was pretty much at the hash mark near our bench ... maybe 30 feet from the basket.

"I kind of flung it up there, and it just happened to go in."

In that moment suspended in time, Remington and Wolcott—two fierce rivals who now were aligned as one—rejoiced together, eliminating the nasty friction that was a part of this consolidation.

"The two towns came together," Mathew said. "I think our basketball team being successful just kind of did away with that whole attitude. After that shot went in, I remember looking up, and that whole side of the Wolcott gym—all the Tri-County fans—ran onto the floor.

"I think our team was on the floor probably half an hour before we went back into the locker room."

Mathew's game-winning shot gave him 13 points for the night. He averaged 17 during the 1971-72 season. Teammate Len Fulkerson led Tri-County with 23 in its victory against Harrison.

After graduation from Tri-County, Mathew accepted an offer to play baseball at Ball State University. He also became fascinated with golf and now is the head professional at the Lafayette Country Club.

"To me, the interesting thing about that night wasn't so much my shot, but just how the two communities came together," Mathew said. "When it was learned that there was going to be a consolidation, there was an injunction filed about how many kids were going to show up from Remington because their parents didn't want the schools together. This basketball thing kind of blended the communities in a sense."

"Parked" in a Zone

No Indiana high school has won more boys' basketball state championships than Muncie Central's eight. The Bearcats are to Hoosier Hysteria what UCLA, Duke, Kentucky or Kansas are to the NCAA tournament.

But in March 1972, one of Muncie's finest teams literally was stunned in its own sectional's title game by tiny Delaware County school Yorktown, which was led by a floppy-haired senior guard named Bruce Parkinson.

Parkinson, who went on to become Purdue's career assists leader, scored 36 points in Yorktown's dramatic 70-65 sectional title game victory against Muncie Central.

"Playing Muncie Central, you just assume that you are going to get beat again," Parkinson said. "They were ranked No. 7. They were tall. They were deep. And they had an excellent player in forward Tim Kuzma. We thought it might be just like any other game against the Bearcats in the Muncie Fieldhouse.

"But we played really well ... great defense. We had a play—we called it No. 4 and it was a back-door play. The forward on my side would go back-door and clear out. I was supposed to reverse the ball, but it gave me the whole side to go one on one. I ended up going one on one almost the whole second half."

Four Muncie Central players fouled out guarding Parkinson, who was 16 for 16 at the free throw line.

"What I remember as the game went on was a feeling like I never ever had before or after," Parkinson said. "It was like it was meant to be. It was just like God was right there on my shoulder. It was a confidence I had never experienced before or after.

"It was like it didn't make any difference who guarded me. I knew I was going to score. People talk about being in a zone, and unless you've ever experienced that once, you have no clue what that means. That was the night I really understood what that meant."

With only a few seconds on the clock, Parkinson and fellow guard Steve Hilton held hands during a free throw situation, telling each other that a miracle just might happen in tradition-rich Muncie Fieldhouse.

"It was like everybody in the Fieldhouse was feeling this thing," Parkinson said. "Momentum clearly was with us. Everybody—except Muncie's fans—were rooting for us. We won, and people went crazy."

In the aftermath, Kuzma lay on the floor in tears. Muncie Central fans were in disbelief. The Muncie radio station interviewed Parkinson's father, Jack, who played at the University of Kentucky.

"It still gives me goose bumps," Parkinson said. "They asked Dad how he felt, and he said, 'That's probably the biggest thrill I've ever had.' That was really special for me.

"The other neat thing was that we went back to Yorktown for a pep session, and people who hadn't been to a Yorktown game in 30 years—along with fans from other county schools—attended. It was as close in the sports world to David slaying Goliath as you can get."

It has been more than 30 years since Parkinson was in "a zone," but he says it's as if it took place yesterday.

Bruce Parkinson—star at Yorktown and Purdue.

"If you look back in your life and say, 'Have I ever done something that nobody else has ever done,' most don't have anything they can ever point to," Parkinson said. "It has always been done by somebody else. That's what has made that game special all these years.

"Other teams have won at Muncie since, but that was special. That was a great Muncie Central team."

Parkinson-led Yorktown followed that victory by defeating Kent Benson-led New Castle in the opening round of the New Castle Regional. New Castle spent most of the 1971-72 season ranked No. 1 in Indiana.

Yorktown's dream season ended in a regional loss to ninth-ranked Richmond.

"But through it all, I will never forget being in a zone against Muncie Central," Parkinson said.

Macy's Peru Parade

Peru, Indiana is a quiet place just a few miles east of Logansport. Its claim to fame is that during most of the 20th century, it was known as the Circus Capital of the World—the off-season home for Ringling Brothers Circus.

It also took on another distinction from 1972-75—the home of basketball scoring machine Kyle Macy, a 6-foot-3 guard who earned Mr. Basketball honors in 1975 before starring at Purdue and then Kentucky, where he helped the Wildcats win the 1978 NCAA tournament championship.

Macy enjoyed an excellent National Basketball Association career, playing for the Phoenix Suns, the Chicago Bulls and the Indiana Pacers.

And like most Indiana schoolboy legends, Macy's story is not a surprising one. The son of Peru coach Jack Macy, Kyle was the proverbial "gym rat."

Kyle Macy of Peru played one year at Purdue before finishing his college career at Kentucky.

Day. Night. Before school. After school. Weekends. Sundays. You name the time, and it was not difficult to locate Kyle Macy.

Macy scored 610 points as a Peru sophomore, helping the Tigers compile a 17-7 record. He scored 680 during a junior season in which Peru finished 12-9.

But Macy saved his best for last, scoring 847 points during his senior year, when Peru compiled a 20-4 mark.

With 2,137 career points, Macy ranks 18th in Indiana career scoring. His 35.7 average during his senior year, which includes a school single-game record 51 points, is the 20th best in Indiana's history.

Despite double- and sometimes triple-team defensive sets tossed at him, Macy sank 800 of 1,625 field goal attempts as a Peru Tiger. He also made more than 87 percent of his free throw attempts.

In the three seasons he helped Peru compile a 39-20 varsity record, Macy averaged 31.9 points a game.

Obviously, Macy was a gifted player, but those who knew him in high school appreciated a work ethic that was second to none among Indiana prep players in 1974-75.

He wore Mr. Basketball's No. 1 jersey proudly and became a terrific college talent and NBA player known for his crisp passes and timely shooting. Macy later followed in his father's footsteps, coaching basketball at Morehead State University in Kentucky.

CHAPTER 3

MODERN
PLAYERS AND
COACHES

The Becoming of a New Era

Maybe it was the bowl-shaped hairstyle. Maybe it was the tiny 5-foot-1 frame. Or maybe it was just Judi Warren's competitive spirit.

Whatever the reason, girls' basketball in Indiana was given the booster shot it needed during the 1975-76 season—the first under the direction of the Indiana High School Athletic Association.

State officials had agreed that 1976 would be the first time Indiana would stage a girls' state tournament—just like the boys in that every school would send its team into the sectional round.

At Warsaw, Warren and a collection of talented teammates that included Chanda Kline, Cathy Folk and Cindy Ross had no idea what a profound effect they would have on Indiana's initial attempt at state tournament play for girls.

Certainly, it was not an easy road for Warren and her teammates. School athletic officials would not allow the girls to practice in the primary gymnasium until after the boys were finished.

Most nights, that meant Warren, who lived in nearby Claypool, would not return home until after 9:00 p.m., just in time to take a quick shower and tumble into bed.

But Warren didn't mind. She sensed that this team was special. Sensed that it could play deep into the tournament, possibly even win it all.

When Warsaw won its sectional, it did so with a crowd of approximately 50 looking on. Attendance improved slightly in the regional, which the Lady Tigers also captured.

By the time Warsaw was ready for semistate play, a curious gathering of 1,500, most adorned in orange T-shirts, followed the Tigers to victory.

Suddenly, Warsaw was Final Four-bound, set to play an extremely talented East Chicago Roosevelt team in Hinkle Fieldhouse, where so many great Indiana male legends had led their respective teams to state championships.

Caught up in the moment of an overwhelming event, Warren and her teammates started slowly against East Chicago Roosevelt, soon finding themselves in an eight-point hole.

That served as the inspiration Warren needed. When the second quarter began, Warren literally took the game into her hands. She made shots. She made bullet passes to teammates for easy buckets. She drove to the basket and was fouled, sinking free throw after free throw. At the other end,

Judi Warren of Warsaw drives in the state finals.

she disrupted East Chicago Roosevelt's offensive patterns by stepping into passing lanes and making steals.

As the game's final seconds ticked off the clock, Warsaw had its victory. Now it would play Bloomfield in Indiana's first state championship game for girls.

Again, it was the Judi Warren show. Again, it was a close game. But thanks to Warren's ability to control the tempo and sink free throws, Warsaw won the state title, hoisting the big trophy at center court.

As then IHSAA assistant commissioner Pat Roy told colleagues, "Thank God for Judi Warren."

The tournament was a success—on the court and at the ticket windows—and Indiana girls' basketball was off and running. Warren was selected Indiana's first Miss Basketball, setting an example for many excellent female players to follow.

Indiana's female basketball talent pool has Warsaw and Judi Warren to thank for its now strong and proud tradition of excellence.

If at First You Don't Succeed ...

Throughout most of Bart Burrell's athletic career, catching passes—not throwing them—was the 1977 Carmel High School graduate's claim to fame.

First as a Carmel Greyhound and then as a Purdue Boilermaker, the 6-foot-2 Burrell was the favorite target of lifelong friend Mark Herrmann—a prep All-State quarterback, an All-American at Purdue, then a National Football

League journeyman with the San Diego Chargers, the Denver Broncos and the Indianapolis Colts.

But on the night of March 27, 1977 in Indianapolis's Market Square Arena, Burrell's pinpoint pass to teammate Jon Ogle with four seconds remaining produced the game-winning basket and a 53-52 state championship game victory against heavily favored East Chicago Washington.

Drake Morris, the East Chicago star, sank two free throws with 11 seconds remaining, pushing the Senators into a 52-51 lead. On the ensuing inbounds pass, East Chicago forced a jump ball, setting the stage for Burrell's heroics.

"The jump ball was staged at the opposite free throw line from where we were shooting, and with Drake set to jump for East Chicago, I knew he would try and tip it backwards towards center court," Burrell recalls. "We had them scouted well and knew that's what he liked to do.

"Just before the referee tossed the ball into the air, I positioned myself in the spot where I thought Drake would tip it. Sure enough, he tipped the ball right to me, and Ogle began sprinting along the right sideline in the direction of the basket. I lobbed the ball over my defender, Jon caught it in stride near the basket and laid it in. We had the lead."

But there was time for one more play, and Burrell, who like football teammate Herrmann scored 16 points in the 1977 basketball state title game, knew Drake Morris would take that final shot.

"There's never been a more intelligent athlete than Mark Herrmann, but Mark, who was guarding Drake, somehow lost him as East Chicago in-bounded the ball," Burrell said. "They easily got the ball to Drake in the left corner, and I could see this horrified look on Mark's face. Fortunately, Drake's shot hit the side of the backboard, and we had our state championship."

Ironically, Burrell, Herrmann, Ogle and most of their basketball teammates expected that state championship to come in football.

In the fall of 1975, pass-happy Carmel was beaten 14-13 by Valparaiso in the football state championship game. In the fall of 1976, Herrmann suffered an ankle injury in the season opener against Indianapolis North Central, and the Greyhounds were beaten, 14-7.

While Carmel went on to win its next nine games by an average margin of almost 30 points, the season-opening defeat kept the Greyhounds out of the playoffs.

"I don't know if we would have won a basketball state championship had we won one in football," Burrell said. "But we were so frustrated by our failure to win in football that we were on a mission during our senior season in basketball.

"We were only 13-7 entering the basketball sectional and had lost our last regular-season game at Indianapolis Ben Davis, but we meshed so well during the four weeks of the state tournament. It's kind of funny when you think about it. I was a wide receiver, and we won a state championship in another sport because of my passing ability."

Lessons of the Game

Bill Banker hits a golf ball as far as the eye can see. And as a collegiate pitcher at Purdue, his 6-foot-4 frame and above-average fastball made him a force with which to be reckoned.

Certainly, Banker's high school basketball career is near the bottom of his list of athletic accomplishments. However, as Banker points out, Indiana high school basketball is much more than scoring averages, shooting percentages and All-Conference accolades.

In a word, it's about life.

During Banker's senior season at West Lafayette High School, he was the starting center for a team that had one returning starter—forward Greg Pond—from its 1979 Lafayette sectional and Lafayette regional championship team.

But veteran coach Bill Berberian, who played at Purdue during the 1940s, was at his best when opponents assumed the Red Devils would be in a rebuilding mode.

Along with forward Mark Filmore and guards Paul Martin and Dave Amstutz, Banker and Pond helped WL become a force late in the 1979-80 season.

Early in the season, Berberian experimented with a two-platoon system in which he would substitute the second five for the first five. As the regular season wore on, the system began to produce the desired results.

West Lafayette was winning. The starting five were well rested, and the second five were happy with their ability to contribute, helping the Red Devils sustain a lead the starters built, or, in some cases, trim points from a deficit.

The second five included guard Mark Rose, the youngest son of former Purdue basketball coach Lee Rose.

As West Lafayette prepared to play perennial tournament power Lafayette Jeff, Berberian decided to keep the two-platoon system intact, despite the fact the Red

Devils would be playing the Bronchos on Jeff's floor—the Crawley Center.

Running its offense as well as it can be run, West Lafayette built an eight-point lead early in the second quarter. It was obvious to everyone in Crawley Center that the Red Devils may have been a basket or two from delivering a knockout punch.

Berberian ordered his second team into the game, and for the first time all season, the strategy backfired. In just more than a minute, Lafayette Jeff countered with a 10-0 run, turning an eight-point deficit into a two-point lead.

Quickly, West Lafayette's starters returned to the court, but after a terrific second half, Lafayette Jeff prevailed by two points, then secured the sectional title the next night with an overtime victory against Harrison.

As Jeff's student body stormed the court after the thrilling victory against West Lafayette, Banker and Broncho center Chris Petty hugged at center court and wished each other the best.

Banker then walked slowly to his team's locker room, where he was greeted just inside the door by Berberian. The next several minutes are ones Banker never will forget.

"Coach Berberian looked at me and said, 'Bill, I am so sorry ... I cost you guys this game and probably the sectional championship,' " Banker said, noting that Berberian regretted the second-quarter substitution selections.

"It speaks volumes about the man and what he meant to me. We lost the game, yet he tried to convince me that it was all his fault. Coach Berberian could never imagine how much he meant to me ... what a wonderful influence he was and how he made me a better person. I spent the next several minutes trying to console him."

Banker said that experiences such as that one are what make Indiana high school basketball such a special part of Hoosier culture.

"I listen to some guys recite final scores and statistics from games they played 25 years ago, and I just shake my head," Banker said. "Honestly, I can't recall my highest-scoring game, nor do I really want to.

"But what I always will recall is that game against Jeff and how much I learned about the true meaning of relationships and life that night. I wouldn't trade that experience nor those moments with coach after the game for anything."

Toran: Triumph and Tragedy

Long before he made quirky Oakland Raiders owner Al Davis smile with bone-crushing tackles from the safety position, the late Stacey Toran earned a place alongside those Indiana schoolboy legends whose last-second shots have won big state tournament games.

Toran, who died August 5, 1989 in an automobile accident in California while a member of the National Football League's tough-guy franchise, was responsible for Indianapolis Broad Ripple's 1980 boys' basketball state championship.

During the Final Four at Indianapolis's Market Square Arena, Toran—a starting forward—and Broad Ripple met Marion in the second semifinal game.

Broad Ripple, which got 24 points from big center Jeff Robinson, led most of the way, but Marion stormed from behind in the closing seconds of regulation, pulling even at 69.

After a Marion timeout, Broad Ripple inbounded the ball to Toran, who turned and tossed the basketball in the direction of the Giants' basket. As the horn sounded, Toran's "miracle" 57-foot shot found the bottom of the net, lifting Broad Ripple to a stunning 71-69 victory.

The two-point field goal—the three-pointer did not become part of Indiana's high school game until 1987-88—gave Toran 10 points in the victory against Marion.

Within seconds after the shot, Indianapolis TV crews replayed it, marked the spot on the court from which Toran launched it, then measured it to derive the exact distance—57 feet.

In the championship game, Broad Ripple faced 1973 state champion New Albany, which brought a 27-game winning streak to the table.

Again, the two-sport standout Toran was a factor, scoring 15 points in the Rockets' 73-66 victory. Robinson led Broad Ripple with 19.

Indianapolis Broad Ripple finished 29-2, including a 10-game, season-ending winning streak. Of its nine tournament games, Broad Ripple scored at least 70 points seven times, thanks in part to the balance Toran helped provide.

In the fall of 1980, Toran enrolled at Notre Dame, where he played four seasons at safety for the Fighting Irish. In the spring of 1984, the Raiders drafted Toran, who played five NFL seasons before his death. He was 27.

An Indianapolis-based children's foundation has been established in Toran's honor—a man who died only nine years after sinking one of the most improbable game-winning shots in Indiana high school basketball state tournament history.

The Fourth Time Is the Charm

Like so many who select high school basketball coaching as a profession, Orlando "Gunner" Wyman learned early in his career that fame is fleeting.

In 1961, Wyman guided Tell City through the Evansville semistate and onto Indianapolis for the Final Four, where Indianapolis Manual ended "Gunner's" first attempt at a state title.

In 1968 and again in 1969, he led Vincennes to semistate crowns, only to be beaten by Gary Roosevelt and Gary Tolleston, respectively, in the Final Four.

So when Wyman announced early in the 1980-81 season that it would be his last, he understood the consequences. There would be one final shot at winning it all.

Vincennes certainly looked the part of a title contender when it reeled off 14 consecutive victories to begin the title trek. But after back-to-back losses to Terre Haute South and Barr-Reeve, some Alices fans wondered if the wheels were beginning to fall off.

Wyman urged his team to return to the basics. Sure enough, Vincennes did just that, winning its final four regular-season games.

It defeated North Knox and South Knox in the sectional, Evansville Central and Mt. Vernon in the regional and Brazil and Floyd Central in the semistate.

"Gunner" was back in the Final Four for the first time in 12 years.

Vincennes coach Gunner Wyman in the 1968 Evansville semistate.

In the second afternoon semifinal, guard Doug Crook scored 30 points in Vincennes's relatively easy 72-53 victory against Shenandoah.

Now, there was only one more hurdle, albeit a powerful one in North Central Conference mainstay Anderson. Again, Crook was on top of his game, pouring in 25 points in a nail-biting 54-52 Vincennes victory.

Wyman barely could contain his emotions in the aftermath of securing his first state championship, exactly 20 years after taking a team (Tell City) to the Final Four for the first time.

The championship was the second in school history. The first was achieved in 1923. Wyman passed away in 2008 at age 82.

Skiles Refused to Lose

Hard-nosed. Gritty. Tough. Passionate.

Select one of the above adjectives, and it describes the way Scott Skiles played and now coaches basketball.

While most know the 1982 Plymouth High School graduate from his NBA playing and coaching career and from his four seasons as a standout guard at Michigan State University, this determined player was the talk of Indiana high school basketball after March 27, 1982.

During that Saturday afternoon and evening in sold-out Market Square Arena in Indianapolis, Skiles literally willed the Plymouth Pilgrims to Indiana's state championship.

Some still say that that three-game state finals—
Plymouth 62, Indianapolis Cathedral 59; Gary Roosevelt
58, Evansville Bosse 57; and Plymouth 75, Gary Roosevelt
74 in double overtime—is the finest ever.

Three games decided by five total points including
the finale in double overtime.

Skiles began his memorable performances with
30 points in Plymouth's three-point semifinal victory
against Cathedral, which got 22 points from center
Ken Barlow and 18 from guard Scott Hicks.

But Skiles—as was the case throughout the 1981-82
season—would not be denied.

The title game is one for the ages, again thanks to
Skiles, who ended that night with 39 points and a state
championship.

Plymouth built a 30-25 halftime lead against bigger and physically stronger Gary Roosevelt, but when
the Pilgrims tired in the third quarter, Roosevelt outscored them 20-8 during that eight-minute window.

With eight minutes remaining in regulation, Plymouth
trailed 45-38. It was time for Skiles to come to the rescue.
The Pilgrims pulled to within 60-58 with less than 30 seconds remaining and got the ball back under their basket
with three seconds to go.

Coach Jack Edison called a timeout. During the discussion, Skiles suggested that a teammate throw him a pass
near the 10-second line. He would turn and shoot.

"I will make the shot," Skiles said confidently.

The rest is history.

Skiles caught the pass near midcourt, dribbled
once to his right and let fly from approximately 40
feet. Swish. The game was tied at 60. Plymouth and
Skiles had new life.

*Scott Skiles (holding ball) in action during
Plymouth's state title game thriller.*

The teams finished the first overtime tied at 65, but Skiles took over again in the second extra session, during which Plymouth outscored Gary Roosevelt 10-9 for a 75-74 victory.

Certainly, the 39 points Oscar Robertson scored for Indianapolis Crispus Attucks in the 1956 title game and the 35 George McGinnis poured in for Indianapolis Washington in the 1969 state finale were dominant efforts.

But considering what Skiles did in making 13 field goals and 13 free throws for his 39 points in the 1982 championship game, it probably is the best single-game performance in Indiana state championship contest history.

Skiles averaged 29.1 points as a Plymouth senior despite seeing limited Plymouth sectional minutes against Bremen and Argos because of a late-season ankle sprain.

The Pilgrims won their first 19 regular-season games, then lost the regular-season finale to South Bend LaSalle 64-62 when Skiles was hobbled by the ankle injury.

In another interesting note, Plymouth won its final five state tournament games by 14 total points, including two one-pointers and two overtime victories. Skiles and the Pilgrims, who finished 28-1, avenged the loss to South Bend LaSalle with a 77-71 victory in the Fort Wayne semistate championship game.

"I worked the Plymouth sectional during that 1982 season, and I knew that if Skiles could get that ankle healthy in time for the regional, he had what it took to lead that team to the state championship," said veteran Indiana basketball referee Tim Fogarty.

"Skiles had an amazing spirit ... an incredible knack of knowing how to win big games. That year, he just refused to lose."

With a four-grade enrollment of 894 during the 1981-82 school year, Plymouth became the smallest school to win the Indiana boys basketball state championship since Cinderella Milan in 1954.

Much like Bobby Plump 28 years before him, Skiles was small-school Indiana's hero in 1982—an Indiana state finals to remember.

Once a Good Coach, Always a Good Coach

Doug Adams always considered himself an educator first and a basketball coach second. To this day, the people who live in and close to Michigan City will tell you that Adams was proficient at each task.

He had an unusual opportunity to prove not once, but twice, that he knew his way around a basketball court.

In 1966—long before Michigan City opted for two public high schools (Elston and Rogers)—Adams had that special team every coach hopes for at least once in a lifetime.

Led by intelligent, high-scoring forward Jim Cadwell and tenacious guards O'Neil Simmons and Larry Gipson, Michigan City compiled a 17-3 regular-season record, including 11 consecutive victories entering the Michigan City sectional.

Adams's team wasted no time exhibiting the kind of play of which state championship teams are made.

Michigan City won its three sectional games by margins of 47, 21 and 39 points. It pounded Elkhart by

31 points and defeated South Bend Central by seven in the regional.

In the Fort Wayne semistate, Michigan City defeated Kokomo 74-66 and Anderson 90-81 to earn the school's first trip to Indiana's coveted Final Four.

Once in Indianapolis, Michigan City never let up. Cadwell scored 23 points in an 81-64 semifinal victory against East Chicago Washington, then added 21 more in a 63-52 state title victory against Indianapolis Tech.

Adams had his dream—a state championship—and soon became an administrator, accepting the principal's job at Rogers High School when the city decided it needed a pair of public secondary schools.

In 1985—19 years after leading Michigan City to its only boys basketball state championship—Adams found himself on the bench again. With two regular-season games remaining, Rogers's head coach, Earl Cunningham, joined a messy teachers' strike, and the team needed a coach.

Adams led the team to a pair of victories to cap the regular season, then watched as Rogers captured sectional and regional championships.

In the opening game of the Fort Wayne semistate, Adams coached his team to a 60-59 upset victory against second-ranked Fort Wayne Northrop. Suddenly, Adams was one victory from taking Michigan City Rogers to Indianapolis for the Final Four.

However, unbeaten and No. 1-ranked Marion—led by Jay Edwards and Lyndon Jones—ended Doug Adams's fairy-tale story with an 83-72 victory in the Fort Wayne semistate's championship game.

Marion went on to win the 1985 state championship, then won in 1986 and again in 1987 to become only the second team in Indiana high school basketball history to capture three consecutive state championships.

Doug Adams returned to the principal's office, satisfied with the knowledge that he certainly had not lost that coaching touch.

Don't Worry, Be Happy

No Indiana high school basketball coach has more state championships rings than Bill Green—so popular that Marion High School's 7,690-seat arena is named in his honor.

Green coached Indianapolis Washington to the 1969 state title, then added five more at Marion—1975, 1976, 1985, 1986 and 1987.

His back-to-back-to-back crowns of '85, '86 and '87 became known as "Purple Reign," honoring the powerful North Central Conference team whose primary colors are purple and gold.

Led by three-year starting guards Jay Edwards and Lyndon Jones, Marion toyed with most opponents during a 36-month run in which it won 84 of 88 games.

But during February of 1987, the chain-smoking Green bolstered the tobacco industry's profit margin. The Giants were winning—they finished 29-1 including a 69-56 state championship game victory against conference rival Richmond—but in Green's eyes, Edwards, Jones and Co. were going through the motions.

"There were practices when we didn't seem like we were having any fun," Green said. "We were winning, but

Marion's 1987 state title team was led by
Jay Edwards and Lyndon Jones.

I didn't think we were playing close to our potential. The kids kept saying, 'Coach, just relax.'

"Funny thing is, they told me later that they were bored with the regular season. Once the sectional began, it was like a new team ... a refreshed team.

"Nobody came close to us. The real Marion Giants stood up to be counted."

Marion's three consecutive state championships marked the second time in Indiana High School Athletic Association history that a school won three in a row. Franklin won three in a row from 1920-22.

It's All in the Words

The bus ride from Lafayette Jefferson High School to Kankakee Valley near Wheatfield never will be recommended as a scenic trek by the AAA Motor Club.

But early in Jeff's 1989-90 season, the Bronchos' varsity used its time wisely while its transportation covered a path through farmland and tiny northern Indiana towns.

Sophomore guard Richie Hammel—the second of former Jeff coach Jim Hammel's four children—not only was blessed with a lethal jump shot, but his academic achievements were every bit as sound as his basketball skills.

Soon after the bus pulled away from the large high school on Lafayette's south side, leading scorer Kevin Whitemen, a senior who specialized in three-pointers, summoned Richie Hammel to the back of the bus, where upperclassmen often gathered.

Whiteman explained to Hammel that he was in the process of finishing a project for his English class—a project that required him to clip vocabulary words from newspapers and magazines and paste them on a sheet of paper.

Whiteman was nearing completion of the project but had had no success finding a magazine or newspaper article in which the word "havoc" was used. Knowing Hammel already had become a favorite among sportswriters who covered Lafayette Jeff's tradition-rich basketball program, Whiteman asked Hammel for a favor.

"You're probably going to score a lot of points against this team, and they're probably going to interview you after the game," Whiteman told his 10th-grade teammate. "If they interview you, could you please use the word 'havoc' in some context?"

Sure enough, Hammel scored 22 points in Lafayette Jeff's easy victory, and yes, writers asked to interview him after the game.

Without so much as a sly smile, Hammel opened his comments by saying, "I wanted to create some havoc with my three-pointers, and that would open things up for our other guys."

In the next day's newspaper, Hammel's "havoc" quote was front and center, and grateful teammate Whiteman was able to complete his English project, thanks to the brainy sophomore whose vocabulary was as prolific as his scoring.

In 1992, Hammel—then a senior—led Lafayette Jeff to the state championship game in which the Bronchos were beaten 77-73 in overtime. Hammel received the Arthur L. Trester Award, given annually to an academically excellent senior whose team advances to the state finals.

River Town Gets Its Title

Sherron Wilkerson certainly was a charismatic figure during an excellent basketball career at Jeffersonville. He defines the hard-nosed work ethic of a community steeped in athletic tradition.

Just a stone's throw from Louisville in southernmost Indiana, Jeffersonville loves its basketball almost as much as it enjoys disliking archrival New Albany, which is just a few miles away on the west side of I-65.

New Albany losses are cherished almost as much as Jeffersonville victories in this part of the state, where many folks live while earning their wages across the bridge in Kentucky.

Still, Jeffersonville is proud to be a part of "Hoosier Hysteria." In 1993, Wilkerson led Jeffersonville as it finally earned the community's first boys basketball state title, clipping Indianapolis Ben Davis 66-61 in the title game, capping a 29-2 season for coach Mike Broughton.

The 1993 state finals were sweet redemption for the Red Devils, who advanced to the Final Four in 1992, only to lose to eventual state champion Richmond in the semifinals in the RCA Dome.

That overtime defeat—Jeffersonville appeared to have the game won in regulation—served as a rallying point for 1993.

Wilkerson, who later became famous after appearing to receive a head-butt from coach Bob Knight while playing at Indiana University, was the Red Devils' leader in 1993, helping a proud community obsessed with sports to its first boys' basketball state crown.

A Beautiful Mind

Whether it's writing a thesis centered on the origin of Western Civilization, or launching a three-pointer from well beyond the arc, Carson Cunningham does so with a creative flair—a zest for life, academics and basketball.

The son of a successful Lake County-based lawyer, Cunningham always was encouraged to be his own man.

While preparing for—then participating in—Indiana high school basketball, this honor student never provided a dull moment.

The 1996 Indiana All-Star from Andrean High School in Lake County wondered if he ever would receive an opportunity to play varsity basketball after an embarrassing moment in an eighth-grade county tournament game.

"I was playing for Our Lady of Grace, and it was a heck of a game," Cunningham said. "Late in the game, I got a rebound, and to this day I don't know what I was thinking about, but I shot a little five-footer into the wrong basket. I scored for the other team. Can you believe it?"

One mental lapse certainly didn't deprive Cunningham of an opportunity to play varsity basketball at Andrean.

A terrific point guard with a lethal perimeter jumper, Cunningham led the 59ers for four years, capping the 1995-96 regular season with a 19-1 record.

During his senior year, Cunningham and Andrean played an inspiring game at twice-beaten South Bend Clay, which won the 1994 state championship.

In front of a packed house at Clay, Cunningham removed any doubt that he was a player with Division I skills.

"I think I had 20 at the half, but the greatest thing was this one pass," Cunningham said. "I was streaking down the left side, and from the corner of my eye, I saw my teammate Eric Coles break to the basket.

"I lobbed the ball off the glass, Coles caught it in mid-air and dunked it.

"It brought the house down, especially the Clay students. Clay put this tight zone on me in the second half, and even though I ended up with 29 or 30, we got beat."

Cunningham's dejection did not last long.

"It's kind of a long trip from Andrean to South Bend Clay, so the coaches arranged for us to have pizza with the Clay team after the game," Cunningham said. "All of their players came over to me and told me what a great pass that was. It's been a few years now, but it was a pretty cool pass."

Cunningham averaged 22.9 points during his senior year and was selected to the Indiana All-Star team.

He received a basketball scholarship from Oregon State, earning All-Pac 10 freshman team honors in 1997.

Cunningham left Oregon State after his freshman year, transferred to Purdue and helped the Boilermakers advance to the 2000 NCAA tournament's Elite Eight before losing to Wisconsin in the West Regional's championship game.

Ironically, upon his return to Indiana and the Purdue campus, Cunningham was reunited with former South Bend Clay standout Jaraan Cornell, whose 30-point game helped Clay beat Cunningham and Andrean in 1996.

Cornell recalled Cunningham's off-the-glass pass, and the two eventually became college roommates. Always open to new experiences, Cunningham planted a tomato garden at the apartment he shared with Cornell, and the two became hooked on gardening.

To this day, they remain close friends.

Now Dr. Cunningham after receiving his PhD from Purdue, he is the men's basketball coach at Carroll College in Helena, Montana.

Fired for the Cause

Those who know 2001 Attica High School graduate Josh Smith smile when reminded that among outsiders, this 6-foot-3 athletic specimen seems too good to be true.

During the 2000-01 school year, running back/linebacker Smith led the Red Ramblers' football team to the Class A state championship game in which they were beaten 29-21 by Adams Central.

Denied a football state championship, Smith vowed to lead coach Ralph Shrader's basketball team to Indiana's Class A title. But with six regular-season losses, Attica and favorite son Smith were long shots. At best.

Complicating matters for the honor roll student was his choice to seek employment in an effort to help his family make ends meet.

Weight-lifting sessions. Homework in preparation for the rigorous academics of the United States Naval Academy, to which Smith received an appointment/ football scholarship as a strong safety.

Toss in basketball practice and a 6:00 a.m. job washing dishes at Wheeler's Restaurant, and Smith barely had time for anything else.

Fearing that Smith had taken on more than he could handle, the restaurant's owners reluctantly "fired" Smith, despite the fact he may have been the eatery's hardest-working employee.

When the sectional tournament began, it was obvious Attica's senior-dominated basketball team was on a mission. With Smith averaging more than 20 points a game in the tournament, Attica found itself back in familiar surroundings—playing for a state title.

Trailing Blue River Valley by 17 points late in the third quarter, Smith took his game to the next level. In less than five minutes, Attica pulled even.

With the scored tied and only a few seconds remaining, the Red Ramblers got the ball to Smith, who was fouled on a drive to the basket. Smith sank the game-winning free throw, sending Attica to a 64-62 victory.

Attica's 28 fourth-quarter points are a Class A state championship game record, thanks in large part to Josh Smith, who was one of Navy's leading defensive players during his time there.

"Someone like Josh Smith comes along once in a coach's lifetime ... maybe," Shrader said. "If anyone ever deserved to be a state champion, it's Josh."

Delaney Hits the Jackpot

Almost a month into the 2003-04 school year, ambitious and hard-working Jason Delaney still was looking for a teaching/coaching job in his native Indiana.

Then one day in September, his phone rang. He might as well have won the Powerball jackpot.

The call came from Waldron school officials, who were looking for a boys' basketball coach and were told that Delaney, then 27, was an up-and-comer.

As Delaney quickly learned, this wasn't just another basketball coaching position. This was a small-school program well stocked with talent but in need of guidance and discipline.

Waldron was 10-12 during the 2002-03 season, but with talented 6-foot-5 twins Justin and Jordan Barnard and a nice supporting cast, the Mohawks just might have the makings of a state-title contender if Delaney could harness their energy.

Delaney could not have scripted a better first varsity coaching experience. In fact, as the season played out, there was no way it could have been better.

Waldron held the No. 1 ranking in the Class A poll throughout most of the season, capping a magnificent 27-0 run with an easy 69-54 state-title game victory against Fort Wayne Blackhawk Christian in Conseco Fieldhouse.

Justin Barnard had 24 points and 12 rebounds, and twin Jordan Barnard added 21 points and 14 rebounds.

That was all Southport High School needed to see.

In July 2004, the 4A school hired Delaney away, impressed with the way he'd turned tiny Waldron into a state champion in one season. Ten years later, after stops at Anderson Highland and Washington, Delaney worked his magic again, winning the 4A state title with Indianapolis Tech, which went 27-2 that season and beat Lake Central 63-59 in the title game.

In five seasons at Tech, Delaney's teams went 79-27. He moved on to Indianapolis Cathedral in 2016-17.

Where, naturally, the Irish posted a winning record in Delaney's first season, going 15-9.

"I can't begin to thank the people of Waldron enough," Delaney said. "They gave me the opportunity I sought, and that's all I wanted."

Delaney's basketball history is well stocked with examples of refusing to take no for an answer. After failing to earn a spot on the McCutcheon varsity roster in 1993, Delaney transferred to Lafayette Central Catholic, where he played for Dave Worland, now principal at Indianapolis Cathedral ... and the man who brought Delaney there to coach.

"Jason didn't have a lot of foot speed, but he could shoot the ball, and he absolutely loved the game of basketball," Worland said. "He was that guy I could put into the game and know that he would not hurt us. In fact, he usually made something positive happen right away.

"When he was looking for a job, I wanted to hire him at Cathedral, but we had a candidate with more experience. But as it worked out, Jason walked into a terrific opportunity at Waldron. I'm not surprised a bit that he won the state championship."

A Work Ethic Unlike Any Other

Brad Lennon got used to the sound, sitting in his office at Park Tudor High School in Indianapolis.

Maybe it was early morning, before the campus of the private school on Indianapolis's near north side started filling up. Maybe it was late in the evening, after everyone was supposed to have cleared out for the day. And maybe the sound was the "thump-thump" of a basketball on hardwood, or some other suggestion of occupancy where there wasn't supposed to be any.

Not that Lennon didn't know who was doing the occupying.

"Yogi," he'd say, sticking his head in the doorway to the gym. "What are you doing?"

"Getting up some shots," Kevin "Yogi" Ferrell Jr. would reply.

Lennon chuckles now, telling that story, because it revealed so much about Yogi Ferrell, the oldest of four children of Kevin Sr., who owns a cleaning company, and Lydia, one of Indianapolis' most prominent anesthesiologists.

"He's so focused," says Lennon, Park Tudor's athletic director during Yogi Ferrell's four seasons and his sixth-grade basketball coach. "Yogi would spend hours upon hours upon hours. He would be here after hours, and I would say 'Yogi, you got to go. I've got to lock the building up.' I know some people that got here before me in the mornings, and he'd be in that gym, shooting and shooting and shooting."

"You don't get that if you don't have that, being ranked No. 1, I don't think," Kevin Ferrell Sr. once told Zach Osterman of Inside Indiana. "It's a long road, and there are a lot of kids who worked hard early on, but they stopped working, and he's just not one of them."

It's one of the reasons Yogi Ferrell—named for his father, nicknamed by his mother—became, at barely 6-feet, a player who stood tall in the annals of Indiana high school basketball. And one who fits neatly into a narrative written by the many celebrated little big men who preceded him in Indiana lore.

There was Billy Keller of Indianapolis Washington, the 1965 Mr. Basketball who stood just 5-foot-10 but went on to star at Purdue and then with the Indiana Pacers, where his 506 3-pointers were second all-time in the history of the American Basketball Association. There was the late Vaughn Wedeking of Evansville Harrison, who at 5-foot-10 was the point guard on a 1970 Jacksonville University team that advanced to the NCAA championship game, where it lost to UCLA.

There was Monte Towe, the 5-foot-7 Oak Hill dynamo who played the point for North Carolina State's 1974 national champions.

And yet Yogi Ferrell might be the best of all them.

Anointed by Clark Francis of Hoop Scoop as the nation's No. 1 player in his class when he was a fifth-grader,

Ferrell bore that weight with a grace and poise far beyond his young years, yes-sirring and no-sirring every adult, never arguing with coaches or officials, seeming to grow calmer as the game or the circumstances got bigger.

And never resting on his laurels.

His basketball IQ, everyone who ever observed, played with, or coached him discovered, was "off the charts." Years after Ferrell led Park Tudor to the first two state titles in school history, finished runner-up to Gary Harris of Hamilton Southeastern as Indiana's 2012 Mr. Basketball, and was named a McDonald's All-American, he awed no less a basketball giant than Dirk Nowitzki of the Dallas Mavericks, who marveled at how Ferrell had the team's sets down cold before he'd even practiced with them.

The best fifth-grader in the nation just kept getting better, in other words. From the day he first arrived at Park Tudor and began to build his legend.

* * *

Everyone knew who the kid was. The magazine had taken care of that.

Yogi Ferrell was barely five feet tall when he arrived at Park Tudor as a sixth grader, but the whole Hoop Scoop hoopla preceded him. He already had a reliable crossover dribble and could shoot on the move and deliver an accurate bounce pass. He'd been hanging around the game since the ball was bigger than he was, watching from the sidelines as his father played pickup games.

Now here he came to Park Tudor, an immaculate sprawl of manicured lawns and low fieldstone buildings on Indianapolis's near-north side, where leafy developments bear gaudy splashes of redbud in the spring.

What struck everyone there right away was that Yogi Ferrell wasn't gaudy in the slightest.

"I think it was very clear when he arrived here that he clearly had basketball skills that were beyond his age," Brad Lennon recalls. "But more than that, he was a really well-grounded young man, very polite . . . We were just struck by his maturity. He was a gentleman, everything 'Yes sir, no sir.' He was not arrogant. He wasn't one of these guys 'Hey, I'm Yogi Ferrell.' It just never came across that way."

It could have. Lennon, a high school basketball coach for twenty-two years, already had the makings of a powerhouse middle school team, but Ferrell took it to another level. Park Tudor's games were never close, which meant Ferrell, and the rest of the starters, rarely played more than three quarters. Many times they'd be up 25 points at halftime.

Before long, fans were lining the running track above the gym floor to watch the sixth-grade team's games. And mostly to watch Yogi Ferrell.

"I think they were upset with me because it was the fourth quarter, and they'd be 'Hey, it's the fourth quarter, where is he?'" Lennon chuckles.

None of those people, however, were Kevin Ferrell Sr. Yogi's maturity and level-headedness began at home, where the senior Ferrell and his wife kept their celebrated son grounded.

There was the period of time, for instance, when Kevin Sr. pulled Yogi out of AAU ball because he felt his son needed a break, and to work on fundamentals with him. And once, when Yogi failed to turn in an assignment on time, his father came down to the gym and told his son he wouldn't be playing that afternoon. And he didn't.

"There wasn't even an argument," Lennon recalls. "But that's what struck us about him. He was such a well-grounded kid, and they had everything sort of figured out. Dad had a fantastic way of putting the kibosh on him. We never saw it, but I'm sure it happened somewhere. He and Dad just have a great bond."

And the son, astoundingly, just kept getting better. All those long hours in the gym, all the getting up shots and instilled responsibility, just kept pushing him to continually raise his personal bar.

"We thought his basketball IQ was so good, and then he'd do something else . . . It wasn't necessarily a pass or ability to score, but his ability to put people in place, and remember and pull out and use some common sense on the floor," Lennon recalls. "It was clear to us he wasn't out there just for Yogi. He was there to make the other kids better."

He'd get no argument from Ferrell.

"I like to think of myself as a leader on the court," he told ESPN one night during his junior season at Park Tudor. "I try to find different guys and give them the ball where they need it. I think I'm a true point guard, and I always want my teammates to be happy.

"I want to lead the team to victory every night, that's the biggest thing."

Not that that was always possible.

* * *

Ed Schilling could see what the problem was. It was Yogi Ferrell.

It was the winter of 2009–10, and he was the new head basketball coach at Park Tudor. It was late January, and Park Tudor was 4-8. Despite all the clamor over this group of players—a group led by Yogi Ferrell and Trevon Blueitt, who would go on to star at Xavier—the Panthers seemed headed down the same path that had produced three losing seasons in their last four, and just two sectional titles in the previous sixteen years.

And it all started with Ferrell—who, for the first time, seemed to have lost faith in his teammates, and was trying to do too much.

And so Schilling pulled him aside.

"Yogi," he said, "until you trust your teammates—until you have faith in them and figure out you don't have to do it all—we're not gonna be successful."

As he almost always did, Ferrell got the message.

The next game was at Indianapolis Ritter. And a new Yogi Ferrell emerged, a Yogi Ferrell who decided he didn't need to score 27 or 28 points per game, as he had been. Seventeen or 18 would do it, plus 11 or 12 assists.

Park Tudor won easily that night, 64–52. It won five of its last seven games. Then it won six more before losing to Wheeler in the Class 2A state championship game, 41–38.

The Panthers would lose just four more games across the next two seasons. They would play North Central, a 4A school from just down the street that had beaten Park Tudor by 24, 40, and 46 points in their previous three meetings, and beat them by 22, 83–61. And they would beat Hammond Noll, 43–42, for the 2011 2A state title and then roll over Bowman Academy, 79–57, to repeat in 2012.

Today, not far from where Yogi Ferrell's framed No. 11 Indiana All-Star jersey hangs alongside state champion team photos from hockey, lacrosse, and tennis, the two state championship banners adorn one corner of the Park Tudor gym. They are joined by two others, from 2014 and 2015.

Yogi Ferrell, who came to Park Tudor trailing accolades that would turn even a grownup's head, clearly lived up to them.

He finished his high school career with 1,853 points, averaging 18.5 points, 6.6 assists, and 3.1 rebounds his senior year. In the 2011 state championship game, he went for 14 points, six assists, and five rebounds as Park Tudor, which trailed Hammond Noll at the end of each of the first three quarters but outscored Noll 10–6 in the fourth to secure the title.

The next year, Ferrell nearly had a triple-double in the state title game, tying a state championship game record with 12 assists and adding 17 points and nine rebounds. By that time, he'd committed to Indiana, and Park Tudor drew overflow crowds everywhere it played, hordes of red-clad Indiana fans standing elbow-to-elbow to watch the great Yogi play.

True to form, the great Yogi never let it go to his head.

A for-instance: the story goes that, at a regional game in Connersville one year, Ferrell drove hard for a layup and then let out a shout. Unfortunately, one of the game officials was standing nearby. He thought Ferrell was trying to show him up. So he T'ed him up.

Schilling, unaware of what was happening, immediately benched his star point guard. At the end of the quarter, Ferrell approached the official who called the technical, trying to apologize.

"You get back on your bench," the official said, or words to that effect. "You're not gonna show me up."

A different player might have said something at that point. Ferrell did not.

"OK," he said, and returned to the bench.

Another chapter in the legend. Another example of Indiana high school basketball's mightiest mite, standing tall.

* * *

Like all his antecedents—the Kellers, the Wedekings, the Towes—Yogi Ferrell's legend just keeps growing. The longer he plays, the taller Indiana's latest vest-pocket force of nature stands.

After opening the door to what could be called the Era of Banners at Park Tudor, he became the icon all those red-clad IU fans hoped he would be in Bloomington, playing in 137 games and averaging 14.5 points, 4.6 assists, and—even at 6-feet-even—3.2 rebounds. When he left Indiana in 2016, he left as the school's all-time assists leader (633) and its sixth all-time scorer (1,986 points).

And he wasn't finished.

Shunned as too small in the 2016 NBA Draft, Ferrell was on the verge of heading to Europe to play when the Dallas Mavericks signed him to a ten-day contract on January 28, 2017. As he has since Brad Lennon had him back in middle school, he proceeded to amaze.

Six days after signing with the Mavs, Ferrell—who started at point guard for the Mavs the day after he signed—dropped 32 points on the Portland Trail Blazers, becoming only the third undrafted rookie in NBA history to put up a 30-point night in his first 15 games. He went on to be named the Western Conference Rookie of the Month for February, and to play in 36 games for the Mavs, averaging 11.3 points, 4.3 assists, and 2.8 rebounds.

"He's demonstrating a real consistency with the level of force that he plays with," Mavs coach Rick Carlisle told Will K. Sneed of *Mavericks Insider* not long after the Mavs signed Ferrell to a long-term deal. "He's showing some abilities as a scorer and as a defender, and he does a little bit of everything.

"He's a guy that we like for a lot of reasons."

Almost everyone has.

CHAPTER 4

SMALL-TOWN TEAMS

The Teacher and the Pupil

During the 1920s and '30s, most Hoosier basketball fans recognized Frankfort as the high school basketball capital of the world.

Everett Case took the Hot Dogs to the state championship game for the first time in 1924, losing to Martinsville.

Case didn't enjoy that experience, vowing never to lose another title game. With the help of some terrific talent, Case directed Frankfort to Indiana's championship game four more times, winning each one—1925, 1929, 1936 and 1939.

Case's 1936 team included one of Frankfort's favorites, Lawrence "Jay" McCreary. That Hot Dog team may have

Everett Case built a dynasty at Frankfort.

been Case's best. It finished 29-1-1—yes, a tie—defeating Fort Wayne Central 50-24 in the finale, during which McCreary contributed six points.

Tipton defeated Frankfort in the season's second game; then the Hot Dogs and Indianapolis Tech played to a 31-31 double-overtime tie. After the second overtime, Case and his Tech counterpart agreed that it was getting late and that the players needed to get home.

After that tie, Frankfort won its final 23 games, including the 26-point drubbing of Fort Wayne Central in the state championship game.

McCreary appreciated Case so much that he decided to follow his mentor into the coaching profession.

Sixteen years after winning a state title as a player, McCreary got one as a head coach, leading the powerful 1952 Muncie Central team to a 68-49 title-game victory against Indianapolis Tech.

McCreary's team finished 25-5, including nail-biting victories against Kokomo (62-60) in the Muncie semistate and New Albany (68-67) in the afternoon game of the state finals.

Jerry Lounsbury's 21 points propelled Muncie Central and McCreary to a state championship that had its roots in Frankfort with Everett Case.

The spacious, dome-like arena in which Frankfort now plays basketball is named for Case, the first coach to win four Indiana high school state titles.

The Hatchets Strike Two Blows

More than a decade after her husband's death in 1982, Georgia Crawley shared what most longtime Washington, Indiana, residents suspected—that the late Marion Crawley's 1941 and 1942 state champion Hatchets were teams the Indiana Basketball Hall of Fame coach expected to win it all.

And the now-deceased Georgia Crawley had an assist.

"Marion understood how much the townspeople adored those boys, but they were so popular that they couldn't find any time for themselves," Georgia Crawley said. "They would walk into a store, and people wanted to talk. They would stop at a restaurant, and people wanted to talk. Gas station? It was the same.

"So Marion told me that we were going to set up camp in our home. I said, 'You mean everybody?' And he said, 'That's right.' I had the whole team in my house for most of state finals week in each of those two seasons. But it paid off. The kids could concentrate and think about the task at hand. Only thing is, they about ate us out of house and home."

Crawley's 1939-40 Washington team finished 25-5 and could have won a state title had standout guard Art Grove not become ill with appendicitis just an hour before the semistate championship game against Mitchell, which beat the Hatchets by one point to advance to the Final Four.

In 1940-41, Washington had plenty of incentive to make amends for the loss to Mitchell. Leroy "Hook"

Mangin scored 23 points in a 48-32 Final Four semifinal victory against Kokomo, then added 18 in a 39-33 state title game victory against Madison. The Hatchets finished with a 27-5 record.

With seven of 10 varsity players returning from the 1941 state championship team, Washington clearly was the favorite to win it all again in 1942.

Evansville Central snapped Washington's season-opening, 16-game winning streak with a 32-31 upset, which the Hatchets would avenge in the Vincennes semistate, 22-20.

Again, Georgia Crawley set up "Camp Crawley" in her Washington home the week of the state finals.

It certainly served its purpose when the Hatchets defeated Frankfort 42-32 and then Muncie Burris 24-18 in the state championship game. Forward John Dejernett had 14 points against Frankfort, and center Jim Riffey had 10 in the victory against Muncie Burris.

After a second consecutive state championship, Marion Crawley requested a small salary increase for the 1942-43 season.

When school officials refused, Crawley interviewed for the vacancy at Lafayette Jeff and stunned the Washington community by accepting an offer to move to Lafayette.

"Had they given him a $100 increase, I don't know if Marion ever would have left Washington," Georgia Crawley said.

Washington's loss certainly was Lafayette's gain. He led the Bronchos to state championships in 1948 and 1964 and to second-place finishes in 1950, 1956 and 1967.

Don't Bet on It

The relatively easy drive from Indianapolis to Cincinnati along Interstate 74 provides plenty of opportunity to engage in lively discussion—in part because the terrain primarily is non-descript, but the basketball roots in that section of eastern and southeastern Indiana are deep and filled with pride and love.

Milan—home of the 1954 "Miracle Men" state champs—is accessible from I-74. They also play some serious ball in Rushville and Batesville, which are nestled in that pocket of the Hoosier State.

But one of the best Indiana basketball stories of all time centers on Shelbyville, Indiana, located just off I-74.

It must be noted that Indiana Downs—one of two horse racing venues in Hoosierland—is based just outside Shelbyville.

That's ironic in that those who like to wager probably would have lost the rent and the title to the car during the 1947 boys' basketball state tournament.

Fifteen games into the 1946-47 season, the Shelbyville Bears had a respectable although certainly not overwhelming 10-5 record. During one early-season four-game stretch, Shelbyville was beaten by Columbus, Lafayette Jeff and Indianapolis Shortridge.

Several games later, unbeaten and No. 1-ranked Terre Haute Garfield handled Shelbyville with relative ease, 52-44. And when the Bears lost to Rushville with five regular-season games remaining, Shelbyville fans were hoping the team could survive the sectional and possibly win the regional.

But timing often is everything. Legendary Purdue coach Gene Keady is fond of telling fans and reporters that "it's not who you play, but when you play them."

In February and March of 1947, no one wanted to play Bill Garrett-led Shelbyville.

The Bears avenged an early-season loss to Columbus, then crushed Greensburg, Indianapolis Washington, Indianapolis Howe and Indianapolis Tech.

A five-game winning streak entering the sectional was just what the doctor ordered for coach Frank Barnes' team.

While most of the state was ready to hand the big trophy to giant center Clyde Lovellette and Terre Haute Garfield, Shelbyville continued to fuel its late-season fire.

A 48-36 victory against Columbus in the Shelbyville sectional semifinals cleared the road Barnes' team now traveled with ease. In the regional, it pounded Madison and North Vernon.

In the semistate, Shelbyville ousted Clinton by nine points and Lawrenceburg by seven, earning a Final Four trip.

Most media members expected East Chicago Washington to defeat Shelbyville in the second afternoon semifinal, but Garrett scored 25 points, and guard Emerson Johnson supported him with 12 in a 54-46 victory.

Suddenly, the Bears were back in a familiar setting—a date with big man Lovellette and the undefeated, No. 1-ranked team from Terre Haute Garfield.

While Garfield was a heavy favorite, Garrett, Johnson and Co. had other ideas. While Lovellette was solid with

25 points, he fouled out. Garfield did not have a second scoring threat to support him that night.

On the other hand, Johnson was red-hot, sinking 11 field goals and finishing with 23 points. Garrett, who also fouled out, chipped in with 21 points, and Shelbyville ruined Terre Haute Garfield's perfect season with a 68-58 upset.

Garrett went on to star at Indiana University. Then, 12 years after leading his team to the 1947 state championship, Garrett won one as a coach—directing a well-balanced Indianapolis Crispus Attucks team to the 1959 title.

Shelbyville's 1947 beginnings may have been humble ones, but at season's end, there was plenty of bite in those Bears.

Who Are These Guys?

If ever Indiana produced an improbable state champion, it was the 1949 Jasper Wildcats, who proved that in sports, timing often can be everything.

For coach Cabby O'Neill, the 1948-49 regular season was a promising team's nightmare. Jasper finished its 20-game regular-season schedule only 11-9, including a 2-5 record in its final seven games.

A predominantly Roman Catholic community in southwestern Indiana, Jasper's roster included several players who asked their priests and nuns to pray for them as they began play in the difficult Jasper sectional, in which the Wildcats almost certainly would have to get past rival Huntingburg.

Huntingburg owned 42-39 and 53-50 regular-season triumphs against O'Neill's team. But in the sectional semi-finals, the Wildcats proved that beating the same foe three consecutive times in the same season is extremely difficult.

Jasper gained revenged with a 44-35 victory, then took the sectional crown with a 48-39 title-game victory against Winslow.

Nothing, however, came easily for Jasper on its unique 1949 tournament journey.

At the Vincennes regional, the Wildcats pulled away from Shelburn but were pushed to the limit to beat Monroe City 57-55 in the title game.

Next up was a trip to the Bloomington semistate. The Wildcats defeated Bedford by eight points, then earned a state finals berth with a heart-stopping 50-49 victory against Bloomington.

Once in Indianapolis, Jasper got 17 points from hard-nosed guard Bob White in a 53-48 victory against Auburn, setting up a state title game with the gifted Dee Monroe and his Madison Cubs.

Monroe was splendid with 36 points, but Jasper countered with 20 from White, 15 from forward Jerome Stenftenagel and 10 from guard Tom Schutz in a 62-61 victory.

It was as if Jasper was destined to win the 1949 state championship.

The Wildcats won their final five tournament games by a collective 17 points—an average of only 3.4 points per contest.

As O'Neill said in the months after Jasper's roll-er-coaster ride to the 1949 state title, "Maybe all those prayers helped us."

Super-Sized Gym

Residents of Dubois County in southwestern Indiana aren't particularly fond of their neighboring communities.

That's partly because high school basketball is the No. 1 hobby and spectator sport for the good people of Jasper, Huntingburg, Holland and Campbelltown.

One legend has it that when a Holland school board member agreed to a consolidation plan with Huntingburg to form what currently is Southridge High School, that board member's barn was set on fire a few nights later.

So, it should come as no surprise that in 1951— after sectional host Jasper defeated Huntingburg— school board members in Huntingburg approved a plan to build a new gymnasium that would seat 6,214.

At the time, that was approximately 75 more seats than people who lived in the community. While Southridge's enrollment varies from 475 students to as many as 500, the school's gym is among the 20 largest in the state.

Approximately 250 Indiana high schools have larger enrollments than Southridge.

Sure enough, the Indiana High School Athletic Association moved the Dubois County-based sectional out of Jasper and into Huntingburg when the big gym was completed.

And when actor Nick Nolte was researching basketball for the movie *Blue Chips*, then-Indiana University coach Bob Knight took Nolte to Huntingburg to see Southridge High School play a game.

The gym certainly has served the county well. Another legend has it that one pair of creative fans seeking admission to a sectional game that was sold out actually totted a 50-pound block of ice to the gym doors, telling ticket-takers that the ice was for the concession stand.

Once through the gates, the fans dumped the ice in the men's restroom and blended into the crowd. Jasper fans claim the prank was completed by a pair of Huntingburg fans. Of course, those in Huntingburg claim the culprits were from Jasper.

Church Street Shootout

Since it opened for the 1959-60 season, New Castle High School's 9,325-seat Chrysler Fieldhouse has been the Hoosier State's largest school-owned basketball venue.

But the huge home of the Trojans never staged a shootout quite like the final regular-season game ever played in New Castle's former home—the tiny Church Street Gym.

On a cold February night in 1959, Kokomo's Jimmy "The Splendid Splinter" Rayl and New Castle's Ray Pavy added one of the most memorable chapters to Indiana's history book of basketball.

For 32 glorious minutes—four eight-minute quarters—Rayl and Pavy literally staged a shooting clinic. Rayl compiled a terrific night, finishing with 49 points. But Pavy would not be denied, sinking 23 of 36 field goal attempts and five of eight free throws for 51 points in a New Castle victory.

While Rayl went on to lead Kokomo to the state championship game—the WildKats were beaten 92-54 by Indianapolis Crispus Attucks—Pavy got the best of Indiana's 1959 Mr. Basketball on one splendid night of high school hoops.

Rayl's 49 points were his season high. His 858 points in 29 games—a 29.3 average—ranks as the 17th highest single-season total in Indiana high school history.

With 114 points in four combined semistate and state finals games, Rayl broke the then-record 106 points set by Indianapolis Crispus Attucks's Oscar Robertson in 1956 and by South Bend Central's John Coalman in 1957.

Robertson and Coalman each led his team to a state title.

Pavy and Rayl each received a basketball scholarship from Indiana University, where Rayl became one of the Big Ten Conference's most prolific scorers.

Pavy, however, was paralyzed during a tragic automobile accident as an IU sophomore.

A Palm Print to Remember

As 1962 Indiana All-Star Fred Fleetwood fondly recalls his senior season at Southport High School on Indianapolis' southeast side, he mentions a 26-2 record, which included a 22-game winning streak, a Marion County Tournament title, a South Central Conference championship and a Southport sectional crown. Toss in Fleetwood's county- and conference-leading 20-point average, and it's easy to understand why the 6-foot-3 forward enjoyed the 1961-62 season.

But one of Fleetwood's fondest memories is from one of only two games Southport lost—a two-point December defeat at Seymour, which was led by high-scoring Larry Shade. Southport was 4-0 when it traveled to Seymour.

"Seymour played us very tough, and we were down two in the closing seconds," Fleetwood recalls. "We called a timeout and ran a play for me ... a jump shot from the right side. Fine. No problem. But I just missed it. It rolled off the rim, and we got beat."

As Southport ran off the floor to its locker room, colorful coach Carl "Blackie" Braden stood just inside the door leading to the dressing room. Braden was not happy.

Standout junior guard Louie Dampier, who later starred at the University of Kentucky and with Kentucky's franchise in the old American Basketball Association, was five steps in front of Fleetwood.

"Braden slapped Dampier's butt so hard that the smack just echoed," Fleetwood said. "We went into the shower, and Louie's butt had the print of Braden's hand ... right on his left cheek.

"We hadn't had a very good year our junior year. So when we got on our bus, I went up to Louie and said, 'Don't worry about it. This won't be the last one we lose.' But as it turned out, we never got beat for 22 more games. We finally got beat in the finals of the Indianapolis regional by Anderson."

Ironically, Fleetwood missed a potential game-tying shot in the season-ending loss to Anderson, whose starting lineup consisted of four sophomores. Fleetwood, who earned a basketball scholarship to Oklahoma University, was one of six 1961-62 Southport players who received college basketball scholarship money.

To this day, that Southport team is recognized as one of the finest Indiana high school teams never to have advanced to the state finals.

He Knew His Stuff

The one-hour drive from Lafayette to Upland along State Road 26 certainly is not Indiana's most scenic, although in the summer of 1963, it provided the perfect backdrop for prognosticating.

Marion Crawley, whose Lafayette Jeff teams won state championships in 1948 and again in 1964, was transporting several of his returning starters to Taylor University's summer basketball camp, which Crawley and Taylor coach Don Odle jointly ran.

Crawley's Bronchos advanced to the 1963 Final Four but were beaten in the semifinals by eventual state champion Muncie Central, 73-71.

Eager to make amends for falling two points short in 1963, Jeff's seniors-to-be engaged in a spirited conversation with their coach as they journeyed to Upland that day.

"All of us felt strongly that we would be among the teams to beat in 1964, and we wanted to know who Coach Crawley thought would challenge us," said Lafayette lawyer Jack Walkey, a Jeff starting guard in 1963 and again in 1964.

"We all thought Coach Crawley would say Columbus, because we knew they had a great team coming back. But Coach Crawley surprised all of us with his response. He

*Marion Crawley coached Washington to state titles in 1941
and 1942 and Lafayette Jeff to crowns in 1948 and 1964.*

said, 'We will play Huntington in the state championship game.' Sure enough, Coach Crawley was correct."

Only Tipton defeated Jeff (72-67) during the Bronchos' 28-1 season, which included 19 consecutive victories after that single December loss.

Jeff breezed through the state tournament until meeting Huntington in the title game. The Bronchos built a 56-50 lead with 5:33 remaining, then watched as the Vikings trimmed the deficit to 56-55 with 1:31 to go.

With Walkey handling the ball, Jeff milked the clock until eight seconds remained, when forward Dave Morrison worked free under the basket, where Walkey found him with a perfect pass and a game-clinching layup.

Huntington proved Crawley to be a basketball prophet of sorts, upsetting Columbus 71-67 during the Final Four semifinals. In the championship game, 1964 Mr. Basketball Denny Brady paced the Bronchos with 17 points, sinking eight field goals and a free throw.

The amazing storyline in Jeff's three-point, state championship victory against Huntington is that the Bronchos played this 32-minute game and made only two turnovers.

Walkey and Brady, who comprised Jeff's backcourt, were Big Ten Conference rivals during their collegiate basketball careers. Brady played at Purdue, and Walkey played for Fred Taylor at Ohio State.

Finally, the Hornets Sing

To completely appreciate the tiny Clinton County community of Rossville's appreciation for basketball, one must understand how much the locals enjoy telling the story about the 1971 team that may be the finest in Indiana small-school history.

On the March morning of the 1971 Lafayette semistate, which was staged in Purdue's 14,123-seat Mackey Arena, local and county law enforcement agencies were concerned.

As the locals tell it, police feared a bank robbery or private home theft.

That's because almost everyone in Rossville was making the 20-mile trip west on IN S.R. 26 to watch the Hornets play in the semistate.

Fortunately, no major crime took place. One lawman at that time joked it was because "even the bad guys went to Lafayette."

Led by John Kamstra, brother Garry Kamstra, Tom Bonebrake and Bob Knapp, the 1971 Rossville team shocked Lafayette Jeff in the afternoon game, then led No. 1-ranked and eventual state champion East Chicago Washington at halftime of the semistate finale.

While the bigger, stronger and faster Senators were too much during the second half—East Chicago Washington rallied for a 79-67 victory—Rossville impressed the entire state.

Knapp, now the athletic director at Rossville, knew that once the Indiana High School Athletic Association converted to a multiple-class tournament beginning with the 1997-98 school year, it would be only a matter of time before Rossville captured a Class A state title.

"There's no football here," Knapp said of Rossville. "The kids, the parents and the fans live for basketball season."

Sure enough, Rossville struck gold in 2002, defeating third-ranked Barr-Reeve 79-68 in the title game in Conseco Fieldhouse. Center Brock Graves capped an excellent career with 37 points, and guard Justin Chittick added 24.

Rossville shot 55.6 percent from the field during a blistering first half in which it built a 45-26 lead. While Barr-Reeve made a second-half charge, there was no catching the second-ranked Hornets, who finished 23-4.

Knapp, a starting guard for the 1971 Rossville team that sent a pair of players to college on Division I basketball scholarships, fought back tears after Rossville's 2002 state title.

"I'd never trade the experience we had in 1971 ... playing East Chicago Washington for the semistate championship," Knapp said. "But to see the people of this town finally watch Rossville win a state championship is something money can't buy."

A Spartan Effort

The best player frequently sang the National Anthem before home games. The leading rebounder and his younger brother always were feuding about the Purdue and Indiana University rivalry, and the bench was a short one.

All the makings for an Indiana state champion, right?

Well, when the subject is the 1972 Connersville Spartans, those elements were more than enough to produce a crown in what became a bizarre Final Four atmosphere at Indiana University's Assembly Hall in Bloomington.

To start with, the 1972 IHSAA state finals were the first of three played on IU's campus, ending the tradition of staging the Final Four in tradition-rich Hinkle Fieldhouse on the Butler University campus in Indianapolis.

While Connersville entered the Final Four with a 12-game winning streak and tournament victories of 17, 32, 57, 22, 23, eight and 18 points, most experts believed that either semifinal opponent Jeffersonville or probable title game participant Gary West had too much for the Indianapolis semistate champs.

After all, while coach Myron Dickerson's starting five was a gifted group led by eventual 1972 Mr. Basketball Phil Cox, some called Connersville "The Five Spartans."

Cox, by the way, could carry a tune as well as anyone who ever has played high school ball in Indiana. Center Gerald Thomas, who signed to play at Purdue much to the displeasure of younger brother Nate, was a quiet man who let his scoring and rebounder do his talking.

Forward Jerry Ellis was a "garbage man," picking up weakside rebounds and laying the ball into the basket.

And Connersville's guards—glasses-wearing Gary Redelman and lefty Larry Miller—had a terrific knack for drawing falls.

On March 18, 1972, this Indiana high school version of the "Fab Five" went to work, finding a way to outlast Jeffersonville 76-69 in double overtime.

Connersville led by seven points entering the fourth quarter, but Jeffersonville charged back, pulling even at 65 at the end of regulation. Each team scored four points in the first extra session, then Connersville outscored the Red Devils 7-0 in the second overtime.

Thomas (19), Redelman (18) and Ellis (17) combined for 54 of Connersville's 76 points in the semifinal victory. The Spartans used only seven players, with Charles Ford and Jim Free playing sparingly.

As Connersville prepared to play deep and quick Gary West in the championship game, Dickerson knew his team would be tired. It played the second semifinal game and enjoyed only three hours' rest between games.

Dickerson knew a fast start would be needed, and that's just what Connersville got, thanks to immediate foul trouble encountered by Gary West.

The foul situation—Gary West would be whistled for 31 to Connersville's nine by game's end—infuriated West coach Ivory Brown, who was whistled for two technical fouls early in the third quarter with Connersville leading, 46-38.

Brown thought he had been ejected and left the playing floor for more than a minute, only to return after being informed that the official was waving him to the bench, not to the locker room.

Each time Gary West made a move, Connersville would draw a foul and step to the free throw line. The Spartans sank 32 title game free throws in their 80-63 upset victory. Miller made 16 free throws, finishing with 26 points. Six Gary West players finished the game with four or five personal fouls.

Casting fatigue to the wayside, Dickerson used his starting five for all but a few seconds, inserting backup guard Free for a tiring Redelman, who supported Miller with 20 points.

For the day, Connersville averaged 78 points, thanks to a total of 56 made free throws.

Troy Lewis (No. 23) was a star at Anderson.

In the aftermath of the loss, disgruntled Gary West fans and supporters of other teams engaged in several fist-fights in the parking lots surrounding the Assembly Hall.

After an investigation, the IHSAA issued a stern reprimand to Gary West and to Coach Brown, whose courtside antics created lots of passion among fans from each team.

Years later, Brown said he deeply regretted what happened, noting that Connersville played a terrific championship game with limited numbers.

Eleven years later, Connersville won its second unexpected state championship, upsetting Troy Lewis-led Anderson 63-62 in a terrific title game, during which Lewis scored 34 points.

But as much as Connersville fans enjoyed the 1983 title, the one its "Five-Man Band" won in 1972 remains the prize to most, simply because so few made so much of every opportunity.

Wins and Wins and Wins

It's probably appropriate that the Argos High School basketball team's mascot is a dragon.

The tiny school just south of South Bend was on fire from February 4, 1978 through December 12, 1981, when it won an Indiana state record 76 consecutive regular-season games.

Madison held the previous record of 61 in a row, established from 1960 through 1962. But Madison is a larger community with a larger enrollment. And Madison had several state finals appearances, including a crown in 1950.

But tiny Argos? The population is approximately 1,500, and the enrollment is approximately 250.

However, in four glorious seasons, Argos compiled an overall record of 93-4. The 1979 club was coach Phil Weybright's best, stunning big schools Elkhart Central, Fort Wayne Harding and tradition-rich Marion on its way to the Final Four.

Guard Mark Malone made two free throws with seven seconds remaining to give Argos a 66-64 Fort Wayne semistate afternoon game victory against Fort Wayne Harding, and then Bill O'Dell rebounded a missed shot and laid it in at the final buzzer to beat Marion, 84-83.

Doug Jennings and O'Dell each averaged 17 points a game for the 1979 Argos team which took a 28-0 record to the Final Four in Indianapolis, where the Anderson Indians ended the Dragons pursuit of a state title.

However, the regular-season winning streak still was intact, and it lasted into December of 1981, when Glenn defeated Argos 58-50 on December 17.

More than 30 players were a part of Argos's amazing streak, which stands to this day.

The Marshall County-based Dragons never have approached that level of success again, but the passion for basketball and the memories from the late 1970s and early 1980s are what Indiana's basketball legends are all about.

A Wigwam to Cherish

If any fan understands the history that is Anderson High School basketball and its beloved Wigwam, it's Doug Griffiths.

In 1983, Griffiths was an Anderson High School junior who was convinced that classmate Troy Lewis would lead coach Norm Held's Indians to the school's first state championship since the 1946 "Jumpin' Johnny" Wilson-led Indians won it all.

Griffiths was more convinced that Anderson would win after Lewis, who went on to star at Purdue, scored 42 points in an incredible 89-87 double-overtime victory against Marion in the Final Four semifinals. Marion's James Blackmon scored 52 points in defeat.

But in the title game—despite 34 points from Lewis—Connersville shocked Anderson, 63-62. Griffiths was stunned.

The Anderson senior-to-be was more shocked in the spring, when he learned that his family would be moving to Indianapolis and that he would attend North Central High School during his senior year.

"I was an Anderson fan, and by the end of our senior year, my new friends were Anderson fans, too," said Griffiths, who made the 30-mile trek from Indianapolis to the Wigwam many times during his senior year.

And when he couldn't get to an Anderson game, he would call a friend or relative in Anderson and have that person place the phone next to the radio so he could listen to the play-by-play broadcast.

While Griffiths again was disappointed when Lewis-led Anderson was beaten in the 1984 Lafayette semistate by Lake Central, he took pride in having converted some Indianapolis North Central students into Anderson fans.

"At first, they wouldn't believe me when I told them how special it is to attend an Anderson game in the Wigwam," Griffiths said. "But once they'd gone one time, they loved it ... really got into it. Anderson is a special place for basketball."

Sadly, it no longer is. The iconic 8,996-seat venue dodged the budget ax until 2011, when Anderson's dwindling tax base could no longer sustain it. The Wigwam saw its last high school basketball games in March of that year, and is now being re-developed for multi-family housing and other uses while preserving the gymnasium that saw so much Indiana high school basketball history.

Current plans are to make it available for practices and 12 events a year.

The Warsaw Way

With thick glasses and an interesting assortment of sport coats and ties, Al Rhodes probably won't be asked to model for the next edition of *GQ* magazine.

But after parts of three decades, Rhodes had built Warsaw's boys' basketball program into one of Indiana's most respected, including a well-deserved state championship in 1984.

Rhodes showed flashes of his coaching brilliance in 1981, leading Warsaw to a semistate championship before falling 71-62 to Anderson in the Final Four's first semifinal.

Three years later, Rhodes had the Tigers back in the Final Four, led by 1985 Mr. Basketball Jeff Grose and forward Marty Lehmann.

Al Rhodes coached Warsaw to the 1984 state title.

Interestingly, Warsaw lost its regular-season opener to South Bend LaSalle, then won 26 of its final 27 to give the northern Indiana community its first state championship.

Along the way, Warsaw had to get past No. 1-ranked Michigan City Rogers 75-73 in the Fort Wayne semi-state's championship game.

In the Final Four in Indianapolis, Lehmann scored 23 points, and Grose added 22 in Warsaw's 78-74 semi-final victory against New Castle, which was coached by Sam Alford, father of 1983 Mr. Basketball Steve Alford.

Rhodes—then 31—became one of the youngest coaches to win a state championship when the Tigers defeated Vincennes 59-56 in the 1984 state championship game.

While Grose led the way with 21 points, guard Steve Hollar sank two game-clinching free throws in the final seconds. Hollar went on to play a feature role in the hit movie *Hoosiers* as one of "Hickory's" star players.

Rhodes took Warsaw back to the Final Four in 1992 and again in 1996, when standout guard Kevin Ault averaged 30.1 points with a single-game high of 47.

In 2002, Rhodes stepped away from coaching and was replaced by longtime assistant Doug Ogle.

But Rhodes established a basketball tradition that to this day is one of Indiana's finest and most successful.

The Stone Age

It's called North Montgomery now, a consolidation of several Montgomery County schools located on the west edge of IN S.R. 231 south.

During the 1990s, the Chargers won a pair of football state championships and always are competitive in boys' basketball.

It shouldn't be any other way, considering that Wingate is a part of North Montgomery. Wingate's state championships in 1913 and 1914 made it the first great Indiana champion, thanks to its big man, Homer Stonebraker.

"Stoney" led Wingate to a 22-3 record during the 1912-13 season, which was capped by a 15-14, five-overtime victory against South Bend in the state title game.

Stonebraker scored nine points in that victory, but it was teammate Forest Crane's field goal in the fifth overtime that was the game winner.

A year later, Wingate—there were 12 boys in the high school—was back for another shot at the state crown. Wingate beat Lebanon 14-8 in the semifinals, getting eight points from Stonebraker.

Then in the title game, Stonebraker finished his career in style, scoring 18 points in a 36-8 mauling of Anderson, which had beaten Wingate 23-21 during the regular season.

Stonebraker quickly was recognized as the first great individual in Indiana's rich tradition of high school basketball. He was a strong, physical player who thrived when tiny Wingate played schools with larger enrollments.

While Franklin's Fuzzy Vandivier, Martinsville's John Wooden and Marion's Charles "Stretch" Murphy burst onto the Indiana high school prep scene in the 1920s, sports writers of that era compared everyone to Stonebraker.

Montgomery County historians enjoy sharing the story that this team won back-to-back state titles and did

Homer Stonebreaker led Wingate to the 1913 and 1914 state titles.

not have its own gym. Stonebraker liked that fact. He liked doing things the hard way.

Basil Ball

While many old-timers among the ranks of Indiana's loyal assembly of basketball fans dislike the four-class tournament format that was instituted for the 1997-98 school year, it provided the gifted Cass Kings with an opportunity to wear a crown in 2003.

It also provided coach Basil Mawbey one of the rarest opportunities anyone in Indiana ever has experienced. When the Kings defeated Forest Park 57-48 in the Class 2A state championship game in Conseco Fieldhouse, Mawbey became the first man to take three different schools to an Indiana title game.

In 1983, Mawbey's Connersville Spartans upset Anderson in the then-single-class championship game. In 1989, Mawbey's Kokomo WildKats were beaten by Eric Montross-led Indianapolis Lawrence North in the state title game.

Mawbey secured the one-coach, three-schools, three-title-games record when Cass—a school with a four-grade enrollment of 564—completed a perfect 26-0 record by defeating Forest Park for the 2A crown.

Beau Bauer, a 6-foot-3 guard who averaged 19 points a game during his senior season, enjoyed a phenomenal title game, contributing 24 points, 12 rebounds and eight assists for a defensive-oriented team.

Mawbey's teams at Connersville, Kokomo and Cass mastered his complex matchup zone defense, which centers on defenders literally running at shooters.

Friends and foes refer to it simply as "Basil Ball."

During Cass's perfect 2002-03 season, its foes averaged only 36.5 points, 13 rebounds and 5.4 assists.

Only two opponents scored as many as 50 points, and only Western (56) scored more than 50. Cass won that regular-season game 60-56 at Western.

The Kings' defense never was better than it was during the state tournament trail. Cass defeated Delphi 35-14 in the Cass sectional opener, then recorded victories of 14, 11, 13 and 10 points before downing Forest Park by nine in Indianapolis.

Given how well the 2002-03 Cass team defended, it would have been interesting to see how well it would have fared in a single-class tournament. Bauer earned a Division I scholarship fro IUPU Fort Wayne and possessed the scoring ability to complement Mawbey's matchup zone.

But after capping a 26-0 season with a title game victory, the people of Walton in Cass County—home of the Kings—did not care that it was only the second title game on a day when four are staged.

Cass had its first state championship, and Basil Mawbey became the only man to take three different schools to an Indiana state title game.

That's a day certainly fit for a king. A Cass King.

CHAPTER 5

CITY TEAMS

Big Men, Big Success

Hoosiers enjoy sitting over a good cup of coffee and debating basketball's essentials.

Some will argue that without a pair of slick guards—a passer and shooter—there's no way an Indiana high school team can be successful.

Others contend that without a big man, state tournament success will end quickly.

The Archers of Fort Wayne South are proof that there's a lot to be said for having excellent big men.

In 1938, Fort Wayne South's starting lineup included 6-foot-8 center Jim Glass, who led his team to a 29-3 record and a 34-32 state championship game victory against Hammond.

Fast-forward 20 years to the 1957-58 season, during which seven-foot center Mike McCoy was the state's domi-

Mike McCoy of Fort Wayne South blocks a shot in 1958.

nant big man. McCoy helped the Archers to a 28-2 record, scoring 18 and 24 points, respectively, in state finals victories against Springs Valley and Crawfordsville.

Fort Wayne South made it back to the Final Four in 1967, led by 6-foot-8 center Willie Long. While the Archers dropped a 79-70 semifinal decision to Lafayette Jeff, Long's scoring and rebounding skills were responsible for South's first Final Four appearance in nine years.

Those who follow high school basketball in Fort Wayne are well aware that when Fort Wayne South finds a big man, good things usually happen.

Glass, McCoy and Long represent different generations and different eras of Hoosier Hysteria, but they share a common bond—size that mattered.

Big Men, Big Winners

Former Notre Dame players notwithstanding, ask anyone in South Bend, Indiana, to list the best basketball players they ever saw, and the older generation will tab brothers John and Sylvester Coalman, who led the 1957 South Bend Central Bears to a perfect 30-0 season and Indiana's state championship.

A physically imposing team, South Bend Central literally pushed its way through the 1957 state tournament, posting victories of 20, 5, 18, 8, 11, 47, 24, 13, 18 and 12 points.

During the two-game Fort Wayne semistate and the two-game state finals in Indianapolis, the Bears' average margin of victory was 16.8 points.

*John Coalman was selected to Indiana's Silver Anniversary
team after a stellar career at South Bend Central.*

John Coalman scored 24 points in the state title-clinching 67-55 victory against Indianapolis Crispus Attucks, which was denied a third consecutive state championship. Sylvester Coalman added 12 points in the title game.

Forward Lee McKnight had a pair of solid state tournament games, scoring 10 points in a 54-36 state semifinal victory against Lafayette Jeff and 16 more in the finale against Indianapolis Crispus Attucks.

Ironically, South Bend Central's most challenging game was the season opener against Gary Roosevelt, which the Bears needed overtime to defeat 81-72.

Thereafter, the Coalman brothers toyed with most opponents, providing a lethal combination of scoring and brute force.

Coach Elmer McCall told friends after that season that a 24-point victory against 1958 state champion Fort Wayne South in the 1957 Fort Wayne semistate, coupled with the title game victory against 1955 and 1956 state champ Indianapolis Crispus Attucks, solidified that South Bend Central team as one of the state's best ever.

South Bend Central—no longer a high school—just missed another state title in 1963, falling to Muncie Central 65-61 in the final game.

Life After Oscar

From time to time, a sport's superstar—Oscar Robertson certainly was that at Indianapolis Crispus

*Bill Garrett (No. 8) played at IU after helping
Shelbyville win the 1947 state title.*

Attucks High School from 1954-56—inspires those who
follow in his large footsteps.

Such was the case for the 1958-59 Tigers, who
found ways to win close tournament game after close
tournament game on their way to the school's third
state championship in five seasons.

With first-year coach Bill Garrett leading the way,
Attucks posted a solid 16-5 regular-season record, but
a pair of those losses were administered by talented
Indianapolis Shortridge, which was favored to win the
Indianapolis sectional staged at Hinkle Fieldhouse on
the Butler University campus.

Shortridge smacked Attucks 59-45 in the City
Tournament and also defeated the Tigers 61-58 in a regular-season game.

Sure enough, the foes would meet for a third time in the Indianapolis Sectional semifinals. Shortridge led by three points with 1:19 to play, but Attucks rallied for a 63-62 triumph. In the sectional finale, the Tigers held on for a 78-58 victory against Indianapolis Tech.

After breezing through the Indianapolis Regional the following week, Attucks used its terrific rebounding skills to defeat Madison 82-80 in overtime and top-ranked Muncie Central 64-62 in a pair of Indianapolis semistate thrillers.

Having posted a one-point victory and a pair of two-point thrillers on their way to the state finals, Garrett's Tigers destroyed Logansport 76-50 to advance to the championship game in which they crushed Jimmy Rayl-led Kokomo 92-54.

Having hung for dear life in sectional and semi-state action, Attucks won its state finals games by an average of 27 points, wrapping up a 26-5 season.

Forward Bobby Edmonds, who grew up admiring Robertson and Attucks' 1955 and '56 state champions, led the way during the finals, scoring 15 points against Logansport and 19 in the title game victory against Kokomo.

Attucks was an extremely balanced team. Four players scored in double figures in the Logansport game and five scored 11 points or more against Kokomo.

For Garrett, it was a sweet "rookie" season. In 1947, he led Shelbyville to the state title as a high school senior. And 12 years later, he coached an Indiana state champion.

These Senators Had Clout

A favorite pastime for Indiana high school basketball fans is discussing which state championship team is this state's greatest.

Some claim that distinction belongs to Oscar Robertson-led Indianapolis Crispus Attucks in 1956. Others are convinced George McGinnis and Indianapolis Washington of 1969 is the greatest.

And a case could be made for the 1987 Marion team, which capped a run of three consecutive Indiana state titles led by Jay Edwards and Lyndon Jones.

But when most who have been watching Indiana high school basketball for more than 30 years offer an opinion, the 1971 East Chicago Washington Senators receive the nod.

East Chicago Washington was ranked No. 1 in every poll during the 1970-71 season, in which it scored 90 points or more 18 times on its way to a perfect 29-0 record. The Senators scored at least 100 points eight times.

The starting lineup was a "Who's Who" of high school, college and professional sports.

Pete Trgovich, 1971 Indiana All-Star, went on to star for coach John Wooden at UCLA. In the 1971 Indiana state finals staged at Butler University's Hinkle Fieldhouse, Trgovich scored 40 points in a 102-88 victory against Floyd Central and 28 more in a 70-60 title-game victory against Elkhart.

Ulysses Bridgeman, who went on to star for Denny Crum at Louisville, played in the NBA.

Tim Stoddard, the starting center who scored 19 points in the title game victory, went on to become one of major league baseball's dominant closers, primarily with the Baltimore Orioles.

Starting guards Darnell Adell and Ruben Bailey combined for 34 points in the state semifinal victory against Floyd Central. Adell later became the head coach at East Chicago Central.

In 1971, East Chicago Washington became only the fifth unbeaten state champion in 61 seasons. During their nine-game tournament run, the Senators posted victories of 32, 25, 11, 14, 5, 14, 12, 14 and 10 points—an average margin of 14.1 points.

"That team was so good that when Coach Wooden sent Coach Crum, who was a UCLA assistant at that time, to East Chicago to scout me, Bridgeman was the guy Coach Crum really liked," Trgovich said.

"When Coach Crum got the Louisville job, Bridgeman was his first recruit. Stoddard helped North Carolina State win the National Championship in 1974, then picked baseball. Our East Chicago Washington team had everything, especially lots of offense."

Chatard's Upset Shuffle

Indiana's tradition-rich state tournament series is punctuated by a long list of upsets—some more shocking than others.

Given the regular-season result, coupled with the talent discrepancy, Indianapolis Chatard's 62-59 upset of previously undefeated and No. 1-ranked Indianapolis Shortridge during the 1973 Indianapolis Sectional quarterfinals is among the most stunning in tourney history.

The teams met in the regular season's fifth game at Indianapolis Arlington's gymnasium, where mighty Shortridge crushed Chatard, 80-45.

Shortridge's backcourt of Wayne Burris and Chester Dorsey was a lethal one, and forward Curtis Singletary was a gifted combination of size and quickness.

Conversely, Chatard relied on team play and execution with a starting lineup composed of Jim Tucker, Steve Kuykendall, Bill Breitenbeck, Tom Moorman and Greg Jansen. They were assisted by top reserves Ross Unseld and Darrell Mills.

After struggling in December and early January, Chatard began to click as the tournament approached.

And when the pairings were drawn, Chatard coach Dave Alexander learned that a rematch with Shortridge was inevitable.

Alexander, who coached the Purdue baseball team from the late 1970s through the early 1990s, wasn't afraid to ask for assistance in developing a game plan for mighty Shortridge.

"In watching a tape of Shortridge's last regular-season game against Lafayette Jeff, it dawned on me that if we could take away their shuffle cuts, we might be able to control their offense," said Alexander, now a scout for the American League's Seattle Mariners.

"I told our center, Bill Breitenbeck, not to guard their center when they passed the ball to the high post. I told him to back down into the lane, hoping that we could take away some of their offense."

In the days before the Shortridge rematch, Alexander called on old friend George Theofanis, who was the Butler University coach at that time.

Ironically, Theofanis once coached Shortridge.

"George thought that if we hit them with a little 2-2-1 zone press and then fell back into man-to-man on the halfcourt, we might slow them down just enough to control the tempo," Alexander said. "We weren't trying to steal the ball from our press ... just wanted to keep Shortridge from running from one end to the other."

Sure enough, each defensive strategy worked. Chatard controlled the tempo from start to finish, recording a 62-59 upset—one of the most remarkable in Indianapolis sectional history.

"After they beat us by 35 points in the regular season, I'm sure they just weren't ready to play us the second time," Alexander said. "But I don't want to diminish what our kids did that night.

"I gave them a game plan, and they executed it to perfection. We were ready. The funny thing is, we accomplished some pretty special things in baseball, but I don't think we ever received accolades like I did that night. We were plastered all over the front page of the *Indianapolis Star*."

Chatard advanced to the sectional title game before losing to Indianapolis North Central. Chatard finished with a 15-8 record.

"People came up to me after that game and said, 'How did you do it?'" Alexander recalls. "I told them, 'I didn't do anything. The kids won the game. We were ready to play, and they weren't.'"

Chatard registered the school's first boys' basketball state championship 30 years later, running away from Fort Wayne Elmhurst in the 2003 Class 3A title game.

But in 1973, Chatard defeated Shortridge in a single-class, winner-take-all format. On one special March evening, Chatard knocked off the best of the best.

Bearcats: Back to Back

It often is said throughout the Hoosier State that if a team hopes to play deep into the state tournament, it must have at least one splendid guard.

In 1978, and again in 1979, Muncie Central's Jack Moore and then Ray McCallum gave further ammunition to those who are convinced that without a little man running the show from the backcourt, state titles simply aren't secured.

At 5-foot-9, Moore was the smallest player on the court during Indiana's 1978 Final Four, which was staged in Market Square Arena on April 15—three weeks after its originally scheduled date—because of the energy crisis that crippled the Midwest during the winter of 1978.

Moore and Muncie Central survived three overtimes to beat Yorktown in the Muncie sectional's first-round game, then hung on in double overtime to defeat North Central Conference rival Richmond in the New Castle regional.

With each nail-biting victory, Moore's confidence increased, reaching its zenith on April 15. During Muncie

Central's 89-85 Final Four semifinal victory against Elkhart, Moore made nine field goals and 16 free throws, finishing with a game-best 34 points.

The championship game against Terre Haute South was vintage Indiana high school basketball—a 65-64 Muncie Central victory in overtime. Again, it was Moore's show. He sank seven baskets and 13 free throws, finishing his high school career with 27 points.

Terre Haute South's Rich Wilson sank a shot from the 10-foot line as time expired in regulation, tying the score at 62. But Moore, who led the Bearcats to a 27-3 record, calmly restored order and momentum, and Muncie Central prevailed by a single point, after which Moore received the Arthur L. Trester Award for scholarship, citizenship and athletic excellence.

With Moore off to the University of Nebraska on a basketball scholarship, it appeared Muncie Central would be nothing more than a bit player in Indiana's 1979 state tournament.

No one, including Muncie Central coach Bill Harrell and his staff, realized that McCallum desired to be every bit as good as Moore. Maybe better.

"Ray hardly played varsity for us in 1978, but I remember that summer how hard he worked ... always in the gym," then-assistant coach Rick Peckinpaugh said.

Sure enough, Muncie Central found its stride late during the 1978-79 season, entering the tournament with a 15-5 record. It beat Richmond by two points in the opening round of the New Castle regional and survived a 47-46 thriller against Indianapolis North Central in the Indianapolis semistate.

McCallum, who has coached college basketball at Ball State and Houston, was determined to give Muncie Central another state title.

In the Final Four semifinals in Market Square Arena, he scored 26 points in a 60-55 overtime victory against Terre Haute South—the same foe Muncie Central defeated in the 1978 title game.

Then, in Indiana's 1979 championship contest, McCallum continued his school's reputation for excellent guard play, scoring 18 points in a 64-60 victory against North Central Conference rival Anderson, which the Bearcats had beaten 86-77 during regular-season action.

During the state finals victories against Terre Haute South and Anderson, McCallum attempted 20 field goals and sank 17—85 percent.

Of note, Moore averaged 30.5 points in the Bearcats' two 1978 state finals games, and McCallum averaged 22 a game in the 1979 state finals.

Two guards whose last names began with the letter "M"—"M" as in Muncie.

Two state championships. The loyal followers of the purple- and white-clad Bearcats say it was destiny.

Harrell, who died during the summer of 2004 in a tragic fishing accident, put it in more basic terms after the 1979 title game.

"We were blessed with two guards who were just damned good," the cigar-chewing Harrell said with a grin.

Sadly, Moore never saw Muncie Central win another state title, passing away in an airplane crash in the early 1980s.

But while neither had the size to post up an opposing guard, their skills and smarts still have residents of

Delaware County talking about Muncie Central's back-to-back state championships of 1978 and 1979.

Terre Haute: So Close, Yet So Far

If ever an Indiana community thinks it is due to win a boys basketball state championship, it is the Vigo County city of Terre Haute.

Terre Haute-based high schools have produced many terrific players, but in 13 Final Four appearances—four by Gerstmeyer, four by South, three by Garfield and two by Wiley—from 1922 through 1991, the community never won a state title.

Center Clyde Lovellette, who went on to star collegiately at Kansas, led Terre Haute Garfield to a perfect record heading into the 1947 state championship game, only to fall to Shelbyville (68-58) despite 25 points from Lovellette.

Bobby "Slick" Leonard, who helped Indiana University capture the 1953 NCAA championship, played at Terre Haute Tech, which became Terre Haute Gerstmeyer.

Leonard went on to coach the Indiana Pacers and now is the color analyst for Pacers' radio broadcasts.

Terry Dischinger was a star at Terre Haute Garfield before earning Olympic gold in 1960 and All-American honors at Purdue. Dischinger also played in the NBA.

"Cam" Cameron, who coached Indiana's football program during the late 1990s and into the 21st century, made three consecutive Final Four playing appearances with Terre

Haute South in 1977, 1978 and 1979, including a runner-up finish to Muncie Central in 1978.

But Terre Haute's real dynasty was coach Howard Sharpe's Gerstmeyer teams of 1953, 1954, 1956 and 1957. During that five-year period, the Black Cats earned four Final Four berths.

Twins Arley and Harley Andrews and Howard Dardeen were Gerstmeyer's top guns during the 1950s. The Black Cats came oh so very close in 1953, losing a state title to what some call "a clerical error."

Early in the game, a referee called a foul on Harley Andrews, who wore No. 43, but the scorer assigned the foul to No. 34, which was worn by Arley Andrews.

Sharpe protested when the second foul was charged to Arley, but the official would not correct the error. The mistake proved more than costly.

With 7:32 remaining in the state title game against South Bend Central, Arley Andrews "fouled out" with what technically was only his fourth foul.

Arley, who was Gerstmeyer's finest perimeter shooter, finished with only six points.

Identical twin Harley attempted to keep the Black Cats in the game, finishing with 20 points. But when his jumper from the top of the key with three seconds remaining bounced off the back of the rim, South Bend Central had a 42-41 victory.

In 1954, state champ Milan defeated Gerstmeyer in a Final Four semifinal, and in 1956 and again in 1957, Indianapolis Crispus Attucks kept Gerstmeyer from the title game with semifinal victories against the Black Cats.

Sharpe, who recorded 755 Indiana high school basketball coaching victories, secured 120 of them during the four seasons in which Gerstmeyer advanced to the Final Four.

Neither Gerstmeyer nor Sharpe ever celebrated a state title, consolidating after the 1971 school year.

Garfield was runner-up in 1922, joining Garfield of 1947, Gerstmeyer of 1953 and South of 1978 as Terre Haute schools to place second in the state finals.

Wiley reached the Final Four in 1924 and 1931 but was beaten in the semifinals. Garfield was beaten by South Bend Central in the 1963 Final Four semifinals, and South dropped semifinal decisions in 1977, 1979, and 1991.

While Larry Bird enhanced Terre Haute's basketball reputation by leading Indiana State to the 1979 NCAA tournament's championship game against Magic Johnson-led Michigan State, the Sycamores came up short in the finale.

Sad as it is for the people who support basketball in Terre Haute, the community has earned a reputation as a designated bridesmaid, but never a bride.

Finally, a Title

Another long three-pointer or two, and Richmond residents would be Buckeyes, not Hoosiers.

But don't think for a minute that this sports-crazy community just off I-70 in far eastern Indiana wants anything to do with Ohio. These people are all Indiana all of the time.

That's why loyal Richmond High School fans were so appreciative in 1992 when their beloved Red Devils finally delivered the most coveted prize of all—a boys' basketball state championship.

So close so many times before, but never a championship.

That ended with a 77-73 overtime victory against Lafayette Jeff in the 1992 title game staged at Indianapolis' RCA Dome.

Chad Austin, who went on to become one of the greatest scorers in Purdue University history, was the catalyst of Richmond's 1992 champions, who compiled a 24-5 record, including an overtime thriller against Jeffersonville in the Final Four's opening semifinal contest.

George Griffith, who built a dominant program at South Bend LaSalle before moving onto Richmond, coached the Red Devils to the title.

Griffith joked after the 1992 title game that "maybe we aren't jinxed after all."

From 1935 until 1992, Richmond fans wondered if there indeed was a curse on their boys' basketball program.

In 1935, terrific guard J.C. "Sam" Lyboult led Richmond to the Final Four and scored an almost unheard-of—at that time—18 points in a 33-28 semifinal loss to Jeffersonville.

Lyboult returned home with the Final Four's Gimbel Medal for scholarship, citizenship and athletic ability, but the Red Devils came up empty in their title quest.

In 1953, mighty Lamar Lundy, who went on to star in the National Football League as a member of the Los Angeles Rams' "Fearsome Foursome" defensive front, was Richmond's high-scoring center.

The Lundy-led Red Devils advanced to the state finals, but Lundy was limited to 10 points and Terre Haute Gerstmeyer pulled away for a 48-40 semifinal victory.

The 1960s and 1970s were frustrating decades for Richmond basketball.

Splendid players such as Rick Risinger, Trent Smock and Rick Thalls annually led the Red Devils into tournament play with an eye-opening record, but the New Castle Regional and the Indianapolis semistate took their toll on the North Central Conference power.

Then, Woody Austin arrived on the scene for the 1984-85 season, and Richmond had the elite player it needed to return to the Final Four.

However, Austin's freshman, sophomore and junior seasons coincided with Marion's "Purple Reign"— three consecutive state championships for the Giants.

In 1985 and again in 1987, Austin led Richmond to the state championship game, only to be beaten by Jay Edwards, Lyndon Jones and the rest of those gifted Marion players.

Marion denied Richmond a state title in 1985 with a 74-67 title game victory. In 1987, Marion pulled away for a 69-56 triumph in the championship game.

Red Devil fans were optimistic in 1988, which was Woody Austin's senior year. Marion's stars had gone onto college, and Austin was the state's best player, averaging 33.2 points.

However, Richmond failed to make a third Final Four trip in four years.

Maybe, some said, it's just not meant to be.

But thanks to Chad Austin—Woody's younger brother—Richmond finally cut down the nets in 1992, quenching the community's thirst for a boys' basketball state championship trophy.

They Play Basketball, Too

No Indiana high school has dominated the state's five-class football state tournament like coach Dick Dullaghan's Indianapolis Ben Davis Giants.

Beginning with the Class 5A (big school) tournament of 1987, Ben Davis played in the state championship game nine times in 16 seasons, winning 5A crowns seven times—1987, 1988, 1990, 1991, 1999, 2001 and 2002. The purple- and white-clad Giants were runners-up in 1992 and again in 1996.

During that same period, the big school on the city's near west side also played some serious basketball, especially in 1994-95 and 1995-96, when Ben Davis became the first Indianapolis-based school to win consecutive single-class boys basketball state championships since Oscar Robertson-led Indianapolis Crispus Attucks in 1955 and again in 1956.

Ben Davis coach Steve Witty's back-to-back crowns were accomplished in stark contrast.

The 1994-95 team was ranked No. 1, led by Mr. Basketball Damon Frierson and dominating center Courtney James. After an early-season loss to Warsaw, Ben Davis was a machine, bringing a 23-game winning streak to the Final Four.

In the state championship game against No. 2 Merrillville, Frierson scored 25 points, and James added 17 points and 11 rebounds, helping the Giants post a hard-fought 58-57 victory.

James sank two pressure-packed free throws with 11 seconds remaining, extending the Ben Davis lead to 58-54.

A Merrillville three-pointer just ahead of the final buzzer created a one-point margin of victory for the Giants.

No one expected Ben Davis to be a factor in the 1996 state tournament. Frierson and James had moved on to college, and the Giants—pardon the expression—lacked size.

Witty had a difficult time settling on a starting line-up, and while Ben Davis' 14-6 regular-season record was solid, there were many teams with stronger credentials entering the 1996 tourney.

But in sports, timing often is everything. As February turned into March, Ben Davis' timing was near perfect. It crushed Indianapolis Ritter to win the sectional, then held off Indianapolis Lawrence North by five points to win the school's fifth consecutive Indianapolis regional.

In the semistate, Ben Davis knocked off a pair of North Central Conference powers—New Castle and Anderson—to secure its third state finals berth in four years.

After rallying for a 61-53 Final Four semifinal victory against Lafayette Jeff, Ben Davis met No. 1-ranked New Albany in a state championship game for the ages.

New Albany seized control in the early moments, and Ben Davis spent the next 27 minutes climbing out of the early hole in which it had been placed.

The game was tied at the end of regulation. One overtime wouldn't be enough, either.

With only three seconds remaining in the second overtime period, Ben Davis guard Keith Patterson spotted guard Jeff Poisel open behind the three-point line. Poisel caught the pass and let fly just as the final horn sounded.

The ball swished through the RCA Dome nets, giving the Giants a 57-54 title-game victory. Poisel was the perfect selection to take the final shot. A 3.42 student, Poisel also shot 42.4 percent from three-point range during the 1995-96 season.

As impressive as Indianapolis Ben Davis's seven Class 5A football state championships are, it could be argued that winning five consecutive Indianapolis regional basketball championships is every bit as impressive.

The only other team to do it was Indianapolis Crispus Attucks, which won state championships in 1955, 1956 and 1959 and was runner-up to South Bend Central in 1957.

Ben Davis basketball? Not bad for a football school.

A Devil of a Program

During the 1970s, Indianapolis Pike literally had a rural feel about it compared with most Marion County schools. Pike was feeling its way, dwarfed by neighboring Indianapolis North Central just to the east and by Indianapolis Ben Davis to the west.

Pike, however, is all grown up now, a basketball coach's dream.

While the Red Devils always have fielded a competitive boys basketball program, Pike has flourished as a big-school power since the Indiana High School Athletic Association implemented a four-class system beginning with the 1997-98 school year.

In March, 1998, Pike won the first Class 4A state championship, defeating Marion 57-54 in the title game, capping a 28-1 season for coach Alan Darner, led by Purdue-bound Indiana All-Star forward Rodney Smith.

Three years later, Pike was at it again, defeating Penn 56-42 in the 2001 Class 4A state title game. Those Red Devils finished 26-3, led by guards Chris Thomas and David Teague.

And in March, 2003, the best of Pike's three state champions in six seasons ran away from DeKalb 65-52 in the title game, getting 21 points from guard/forward Robert Vaden, completing a perfect 29-0 season for coach Larry Bullington.

Pike just missed a fourth crown, falling to Gary West in the 2002 finale.

In winning the 1998, 2001 and 2003 Class 4A state titles, the Red Devils' collective record was 83-4.

The 2002-03 team averaged 73.2 points a game while surrendering only 49.1.

In winning seven state tournament games, Pike recorded victories of 19, 14, 23, 8, 13, 23 and 13 points. Center Justin Cage led this balanced team with a 13.4 scoring average, followed by Vaden's 13.2 and forward Courtney Lee's 11.4.

While most big schools frowned on the IHSAA's decision to dump the one-class tournament and replace it with four enrollment-based tourneys, Indianapolis Pike played for the big-school state title four times in the first six seasons after the switch from one class.

Needless to say, Indianapolis Pike is rural no more.

CHAPTER 6

FAMILY

The Conner Family Coaching Tree

When brother-and-sister Charles and Martha Conner were growing up in the 1920s and '30s on a plot of fertile Benton County farmland, sports provided the primary source of family entertainment.

Basketball and baseball were Conner family passions.

Charles and Martha Conner, however, never could have imagined a family tree with so many Indiana high school state championship branches.

- Charles Conner's oldest daughter, Jan, coached the Martinsville girls' basketball team to back-to-back state championships in 1997 and 1998 after many seasons as a highly successful coach at Benton Central.
- Jan Conner's 1998 Martinsville team won the first Class 4A—big school—crown after the single-class

system was revamped into four enrollment-based divisions for the 1997-98 school year.

- Charles Conner's oldest daughter, Penny, is the proud mother of Chad Dunwoody, who has coached Lafayette Central Catholic's boys basketball teams to Class A state championships in 1998, 2000 and 2003.
- Chad Dunwoody's 1999 team was the Class A runner-up.
- Martha Conner's son, Steve Dietrich, coached West Lafayette's girls' basketball team to the 1998 Class 3A state championship.
- Jan Conner and Steve Dietrich are first cousins. Jan Conner is Chad Dunwoody's maternal aunt. Steve Dietrich and Chad Dunwoody are second cousins.
- Three members of the Conner clan coached six state championship teams and a runner-up during a seven-year window. As improbable as it sounds, it certainly is true.

It's more improbable when you consider that in 1998—the first year for Indiana's multiple-class boys' and girls' basketball tournaments—Jan Conner, Steve Dietrich and Chad Dunwoody each coached a state champion.

"When you stop and think about it, it really is an amazing accomplishment," said Chad Dunwoody, one of only seven men to have coached as many as three Indiana boys basketball state championship teams.

"I think Grandpa Conner would be thrilled. It's just a shame he didn't live to see it. I know how much he truly loved athletics."

The Conner/Dunwoody/Dietrich family tree has one other state championship to its credit, this one as a participant.

*Jan Conner (right) and John Wooden celebrate
Martinsville's girls' state title.*

Todd Dunwoody, Chad's younger brother, was a star wide receiver for Harrison High School's 1992 Class 3A football state championship team, which defeated Fort Wayne Wayne High in the title game in Indianapolis's RCA Dome.

Todd Dunwoody was the Florida Marlins' starting center fielder in 1998 and 1999 and also has played in the major leagues with the Kansas City Royals, the Chicago Cubs and the Cleveland Indians.

A former three-sport star at Harrison in northern Tippecanoe County, Todd Dunwoody was the Florida Marlins' seventh-round selection in major league baseball's amateur draft of June, 1993.

Fort Wayne's Favorite
Father and Son

Almost every Indiana high school basketball coach will tell you that one of the most difficult facets of the job is coaching one's son.

Fans and parents of other players cry favoritism. The expectation levels usually are set too high for a coach's kid. And being together night and day and day and night sometimes creates cabin fever between father and son.

But somehow—with the world at war in 1943—coach Murray Mendenhall, Sr., and guard Murray Mendenhall, Jr., managed to find the perfect chemistry during Fort Wayne Central's 27-1 season, which included a 45-40 victory against Lebanon in the state championship game.

Mendenhall Sr. was blessed with lots of experienced depth during the 1942-43 season, and he used that talent to his advantage, frequently pulling a player from the game for a brief respite.

For example, in Fort Wayne Central's 33-24 Final Four semifinal victory against Batesville, Mendenhall Sr. used 10 players while Batesville used only six. No Central player scored more than eight points in that game, but balance was the difference.

In the title game, eight Fort Wayne Central players saw action, but Lebanon used its starting five the entire way. Mendenhall Jr. scored 10 points in the championship game while forward Robert VanRyan led the way with 11.

Fort Wayne Central opened the 1942-43 season with nine consecutive victories before Fort Wayne South handed the eventual state champions their only defeat, 26-22.

Mendenhall Sr. then guided his team to 18 consecutive victories to close the season, including a thrilling 25-24 overtime victory against Fort Wayne South in the Fort Wayne Sectional's semifinals.

The Sexson Clan

How often do we hear a basketball fan turn to a friend and say, "Now, there's some serious basketball genes in that family."

Joe Sexson, his son, Rick, and Rick's son, Ryan, are living proof that the above statement can be quite true.

From 1952, when Joe Sexson led Indianapolis Tech to within one victory of the state championship, through 1996, when Ryan Sexson led Lafayette Jeff to the Final Four in the next to last one-class state tournament, the Sexson name was synonymous with Indiana high school basketball excellence.

In 1952, Sexson was a strong, 6-foot-5 forward who scored 18 points in Tech's 56-49 Final Four semifinal victory against Lafayette Jeff. Ironically, Sexson's three sons and two grandsons now are Jeff graduates.

In the championship game against Muncie Central, Joe Sexson scored 26 points, but the Bearcats pulled away for a 68-49 victory. Sexson did receive the Arthur L. Trester Award for academic excellence, sportsmanship and athletic ability.

Joe Sexson then accepted a basketball scholarship to play at Purdue for Ray Eddy, enrolling in the fall of 1952.

In January, 1954, Joe Sexson's wife, Donna, gave birth to the first of their three sons—Rick.

Upon graduation from Purdue, Joe Sexson became the Boilermakers' head baseball coach and an assistant basketball coach, settling his family in Lafayette, where Marion Crawley—whose 1952 Jeff team Sexson had helped beat in the Final Four—still was the basketball coach.

Rick Sexson developed into an excellent high school basketball and baseball player. While Crawley retired from coaching after the 1967 state championship game, Rick Sexson went on to become a standout player for new Jeff coach Joe Heath.

As a senior in 1972, Rick Sexson scored 31 points in his final high school game, a Lafayette semistate loss to No. 1-ranked Michigan City Elston.

Rick Sexson went on to enjoy an excellent playing career at Butler University, later joining his father's staff when Joe Sexson was selected as Butler's head coach.

Ryan Sexson is the older of Rick and Ellen Sexson's two sons. Early on, Ryan developed a lethal perimeter shooting touch, and in 1996, he caught fire in the state tournament series, leading the Bronchos to Lafayette sectional, Lafayette regional and Lafayette semistate championships as a sophomore for coach Jim Hammel.

Playing in the RCA Dome, Ryan Sexson sank a pair of long three-pointers as Lafayette Jeff built an early lead against Indianapolis Ben Davis. But in the end, Ben Davis rallied for a 61-53 victory, denying the Sexson family a state crown.

However, as Joe Sexson says, "There aren't many families that honestly can tell you that in three generations, two played in the Final Four and the other took his team to the semistate."

Ryan Sexson went on to play collegiately for Homer Drew at Valparaiso before transferring to Purdue-Calumet, where he finished.

Carmel's Scoring Machines

Glance at the list of Indiana's most prolific scorers, and the name Shepherd is impossible to miss.

Among Indiana's career scoring leaders, Billy Shepherd, who graduated from Carmel in 1968, ranks fifth with 2,465 points. Younger brother Dave Shepherd, who graduated from Carmel in 1970, ranks 11th with 2,226 points.

That's a combined 4,691 points from a pair of perimeter shooting guards in an era long before the addition of the three-point line.

Dave Shepherd still holds Indiana's single-season record, pouring in 1,079 points during the 1969-70 season, when he led the Greyhounds to the state championship game in which they were beaten by East Chicago Roosevelt.

In that title game loss to East Chicago Roosevelt, Dave Shepherd scored a record 40 points, wiping out the 39 points scored by Indianapolis Crispus Attucks' Oscar Robertson in a 1956 title game victory against Lafayette Jeff.

Shepherd finished his senior year with a 37.2 average, including a single-game high of 66. New Castle's Steve Alford almost shattered Dave Shepherd's record, scoring

*Dave Shepherd (left), Bill Shepherd Sr. (center), and Billy
Shepherd (right) in 1968 at Carmel.*

1,078 points during the 1982-83 season, when the Trojans
reached the Indianapolis semistate's final game.

While the Shepherd brothers laid the foundation for
basketball excellence in Carmel, they never experienced
a state title. However, seven years after Dave Shepherd
rewrote the state scoring record, Carmel won a state
crown, defeating East Chicago Washington in the 1977
finale.

Ironically, the youngest Shepherd brother—guard
Steve—was a role player for the Greyhounds' 1977 state
champs.

The Harden Boys

Talk to the friendly people who call Covington, Indiana home, and two topics will be mentioned within the conversation's first five minutes—boys' basketball and the Beef House Restaurant.

While the thick, juicy steaks, melt-in-your-mouth rolls and gigantic salad bar make the Beef House the people's choice in western Indiana, the folks who eat there most often usually are Covington Trojan fans.

The Fountain County-based high school has had plenty of excellent players during the past century, but with the exception of 1978 Indiana All-Star Dale White, the name mentioned most often—especially by those on the far side of 50—is Al Harden.

Coaches, athletic directors and former players probably know Al Harden as Indiana's onetime king of Converse. If you needed a pair of basketball shoes, or any kind of basketball apparel, Al Harden was the man to see.

But from 1959-61, Harden was one of the most exciting guards in a state that experienced its basketball glory years during the 1950s and 1960s.

Covington won 13 times when Harden was a starting sophomore guard, then hit the jackpot in 1960. Harden and Co. won sectional and regional championships, then stunned Lafayette Jeff in the opening round of the Lafayette semistate.

Little Covington—a community with a big gymnasium and one of the best steakhouses in the Midwest—was one victory from the Final Four in Indiana's one-class tournament.

Unfortunately for Harden, Covington and the many small-town fans who prayed for a basketball miracle, eventual state champion East Chicago Washington defeated the Trojans by 26 points in the Lafayette semistate's championship game.

But cat-quick Al Harden had made a name for himself. So much so that former Indiana University coach Branch McCracken offered Harden a basketball scholarship, which would include the opportunity to play alongside twins Tom and Dick Van Arsdale and Jimmy Rayl.

Harden jumped at the offer, smiling all the way to Bloomington. At that point, Harden remembered when he was eight years old and the people of Covington built a new 3,200-seat gymnasium for the sole purpose of taking the sectional site away from rival Attica.

It worked, and in 1960, Harden and Covington used that home-court advantage to win the sectional championship.

After graduating from Indiana, Harden returned to Fountain County as varsity basketball coach at the new consolidation known as Fountain Central, which included students from Veedersburg, Newtown and several other tiny communities.

From there, small-town hero Harden accepted an opportunity to coach basketball at the University of Denver. But when budding basketball star sons Rob and Roger were closing in on attending high school, Al Harden wasn't about to let them miss out on the "Hoosier Hysteria" experience.

Al Harden accepted a job with Converse, and while he was based out of Chicago, he moved his family to the northern Indiana community of Valparaiso, where sons

Rob and Roger became Hoosier schoolboy standouts at Valparaiso High School.

Rob earned Indiana All-Star team status in 1981, and in 1982, Roger was selected Indiana's Mr. Basketball, edging another Indiana legend—Plymouth guard Scott Skiles—for the state's top individual honor.

It has been more than half a century since Al Harden watched as the people of Covington constructed a basketball temple in which he would become an Indiana legend.

And it has been a long time since Al Harden called Fountain County his home.

But for as long as a Harden boy draws a breath, there will be an appreciation for what Indiana high school basketball can do for a small-town boy who dares to dream big.

From Agony to Ecstasy

It would be impossible to find an Indiana high school basketball player who endured more sorrow on the night before his senior season's opening game than Walter Jordan, for whom sport really didn't matter in November, 1973.

Jordan's mother was diagnosed with terminal cancer during the summer of 1973, just as the sharp-shooting 6-foot-6 forward was blossoming into Fort Wayne Northrop's standout player.

But only hours before the Bruins' 54-52 season-opening triumph against Fort Wayne North, Jordan's mother died at home. In her final moments, she called her son to her side.

"She told me that she was proud of me and that she knew I could lead our team to the state championship," Jordan said. "She also told me that she knew I could earn a college scholarship and maybe go on and play pro ball. I was grief-stricken, but I also was inspired."

Four months later, Jordan and his Bruin teammates put the finishing touches on a brilliant 28-1 season, defeating Jeffersonville 59-56 in the state championship game, which was staged in Indiana University's Assembly Hall in Bloomington.

Jordan scored a team-best 20 points in the state title game after pouring in 26 points during a 63-49 victory against Lafayette Jeff in the State Finals' opening-round game.

"It was an incredible season," Jordan said. "We beat a great Anderson team 67-52 to win the Fort Wayne semistate championship. That was considered quite an upset, because Anderson had Roy Taylor, who was one of the best players I'd ever faced.

"Here we were—a school that had been built only three years before—and we were state champions. I know in some way, my mother was watching over us all the way."

Jordan received a basketball scholarship from Purdue. He averaged 16.6 points during a four-year career and is the Boilermakers' No. 8 career scorer with 1,813 points. He shot 47.9 percent from the field in his collegiate career.

After a brief stint with the Cleveland Cavaliers of the NBA, Jordan played several professional seasons in Europe.

The Scholarship Game

The summer of 1982 was an extraordinary one for Muncie area natives Matt Painter and Joe Luce, fifth-graders whose love of basketball brought them together as YMCA League teammates.

Painter, a lawyer's son who attended Delta on Delaware County's north side, and Luce, a hard-nosed kid from Wapahani to the east of Muncie, became instant friends.

"Matt wasn't the most athletic kid on the court, but in one way or another, he was the best player on that court," said Luce, now the varsity basketball coach at Marion.

While Painter and Luce often traveled in different social groups, their friendship never skipped a beat, even when their high school teams met in March 1988 in the Blackford sectional's championship game.

In one of the finest individual performances in Delta history, Painter single-handedly kept his team within striking distance, scoring 36 points and reaching double figures in rebounds and assists.

But when the final horn sounded, Luce and Wapahani hoisted the coveted sectional championship trophy.

"To this day, every time Matt and I visit, he thanks me for the scholarship he received from Purdue," Luce said. "You see, it was me guarding—or attempting to guard—Matt that night. Obviously, I didn't do a very good job.

"But no one was more deserving than Matt. When we were 12 years old, he was the only kid we knew who had a subscription to *HoopScoop* magazine. He knew of every good high school player in the state when we were in sixth grade."

Painter, a 1989 Delta grad, went on to play four seasons at Purdue for Gene Keady. On April 9, 2004, Painter officially was introduced as the man to replace Keady as the Boilermakers' head coach. He took over after the 2004-05 season and is still there today.

"Bloom Baby"

Grandfather and grandson relationships often create special athletic bonds, especially when the elder gentleman makes a goal-related request.

During Mt. Vernon High School's 1994-95 season, then senior guard Elliot Bloom delivered and then some in a game at rival Lapel.

Bloom, the sixth man but the team's second leading scorer with a 13-point average, set a school single-game record with 11 3-pointers in a victory at Lapel.

"I grew up mowing my grandfather [Charles Bloom's] lawn," Bloom said. "He was kind of my hero. We would watch Chicago Cubs games together during the summer.

"He called me on that Saturday morning and said, 'Good luck tonight at Lapel. I want you to hit five threes tonight for me. When I get my Sunday paper, I like to read about this stuff.' I said, 'OK.'"

As the game began, the rim seemed as if it was a mile wide to Bloom, who never had played in Lapel's gym, which is small and compact.

"It got pretty loud," Bloom said. "I had three or four threes at halftime, and coach Jimmy Howell said, 'Get him the ball. He obviously is feeling it.' The second half started, and I hit a couple more. Then, people started realizing that I was at seven threes. Lapel started getting upset about it. We were starting to blow them out."

On the next possession, Mt. Vernon's Tyrone Garrison threw a baseball pass to Bloom right in front of the Mt. Vernon bench. Bloom launched a trey, and a Lapel player tackled him into the bench.

Bloom sank the three-pointer and was awarded a free throw. Bloom was taken out of the game with 10 seconds remaining after sinking the school-record 11 treys in 18 attempts, finishing with 39 points.

The Lapel fans even joined in the standing ovation for the Mt. Vernon sixth man with the sweet three-point shot.

The next day, the *Indianapolis Star* headline read, "Bloom, Baby," a play on words from Indiana Pacers announcer Bobby "Slick" Leonard, who shouts, "Boom, Baby" each time a Pacer sinks a three-pointer.

Charles Bloom called his grandson early Sunday morning with a simple message.

"You didn't listen to me one bit," Charles Bloom said. "I asked you to get five threes, and here you go and get 11."

"He gave me a bunch of heck for that," Elliot Bloom said. "It means a lot to me because I was able to do it for him."

This One Is for You, Dad

Indianapolis was loaded with talented high school basketball players during the late 1960s and early '70s, including a smooth 6-foot-6 forward from Arsenal Tech High School named Frank Kendrick.

But winning the Indianapolis Hinkle sectional was as difficult a task as any in Indiana high school circles. While earning a spot on the coveted Indiana All-Star team and a scholarship from Purdue, Frank Kendrick never played in the state finals before graduating in the spring of 1970.

Kendrick went on to earn All-American honors at Purdue, leading the 1974 Boilermakers to the National Invitation Tournament championship in New York's Madison Square Garden.

Still, Kendrick longed for an Indiana high school state title.

Leave it to his oldest son, Kristof, to deliver—not once, but twice.

In 2000, then-freshman Kristof Kendrick helped Lafayette Central Catholic defeat Union (Dugger) 82-70 in the Class A title game in Indianapolis's Conseco Fieldhouse.

And in 2003, then-senior Kendrick contributed a team-best 24 points and eight rebounds, leading the Knights to a 68-64 come-from-behind victory against Southwestern High School.

During the game's final 16 minutes, Kendrick-led Central Catholic outscored Southwestern 41-25, erasing what had been a 12-point halftime deficit.

Moments after the game, the Kendricks—father and son—exchanged a tearful hug.

"Since I was little, I remember my dad talking about how much he enjoyed playing high school basketball in Indiana, but that he never had the chance to win a ring," Kristof said. "This victory was for us, but it's also for my dad."

CHAPTER 7

THE YOUNGEST MR. BASKETBALL

Gary Harris was born to the game.

Long before he became Indiana's 2012 Mr. Basketball at the age of 17—before he shot and rebounded and passed and defended his way into Indiana's rich schoolboy basketball tapestry as a two-sport star at Hamilton Southeastern—he was accompanying his mother, a former Purdue University standout, as she played exhibition games with a traveling squad called the Lady Hoosier Stars.

Joy Holmes Harris graduated from Purdue in 1991 as a four-year letter winner and WBCA All-American who still ranks seventh in Boilermakers history with 1,747 points, and she played one season (2000) with the Detroit Shock of the WNBA. And when Gary was all of two months old, she took him with her on the Lady Hoosier Stars tour.

The basketball court was his nursery. The squeak of sneakers and drumming of basketballs on hardwood were his lullabies.

"He started out in a gym and he's always been there," his mom says. "He's always been around it."

*Gary Harris in action during the 2012 McDonald's
All-America game / AP Photo*

Eventually, all that gym time would produce a 6-foot-4, 205-pound guard who, as a senior, was both a McDonald's and *Parade Magazine* All-American, ranked the No. 2 shooting guard and No. 11 overall player in the nation by ESPNU100, and finished his career as Hamilton Southeastern's alltime leader in scoring (1,540 points), rebounding (467, a 5.1 per-game average), assists (232, or 2.5 per game) and steals (232, 2.5 per game).

Then he went off to Michigan State, where, at 18, he was named the Big Ten Freshman of the Year in 2013 after averaging 12.9 points for the Spartans, second on the team.

And yet there was this: In spite of his lineage, hardly anyone saw it coming at first.

A Player—In Two Sports

The news from Columbus, Ohio, that day was startling.

As nearly as Joy Harris can recollect, her oldest son was in "seventh or eighth grade" the day his father, also named Gary, came home to say that young Gary had been named the MVP of an AAU tournament there.

"Really?" Joy said.

"Really. He was great," her husband replied.

"When he was very young, he was not the best player on his team coming up through the AAU circuit," Joy Harris says. "But after that tournament, I started to see flashes of it. We used to get out in the backyard and I could see improvement in his game just playing him one-on-one. I guess that's when I knew that he could probably be a player."

That's about the time his high school coach, Brian Satterfield, saw the same thing.

"We have a little travel program we always do, and he wasn't there in the early stages," recalls Satterfield, who has coached two straight Mr. Basketballs—Harris in 2012 and Michigan recruit Zak Irvin in 2013. "I mean, you always see kids come to you at camps, and we try as a coaching staff to select the teams just to take the biases out of it. When he was doing the travel tryouts, you could tell then. That would have been probably his sixth grade year.

"But I probably recognized him the most when he eventually got to junior high. It was interesting then. People would always tell him he needed to work on his left hand because he would always go right. But people couldn't stop him when he went right so he really didn't have to use his left hand."

By the time he arrived at Hamilton Southeastern as a freshman, he'd become adept enough with both hands to earn a spot on the varsity roster. Within four games, he was a starter; by the time he was a sophomore, he was averaging 14 points, four rebounds, two assists and three steals and leading Hamilton Southeastern to a 17-4 record.

"As he was coming in as a freshman, we saw him having an opportunity to play varsity just because of what he could do," Satterfield says. "First week of practice, we knew he was varsity only. For me, it was just his all-around game that stuck out. You always talk about players that could do this or do that, but for him it was what he did with whatever he did. Shooting, ballhandling, offense, defense, the whole gamut of things."

In the fall, meanwhile, he was an emerging star in his second love, football, where, as a wide receiver, he would catch 119 passes for 2,145 yards and 32 touchdowns in three seasons as a starter.

So enamored was he of football, in fact, that it wasn't really until his junior year of high school that he decided basketball would be his chosen path to college. And even then, he insisted on playing football as a senior.

"People were saying 'Why are you doing this?'" says his mom. "And he said, 'Because I love football.' I mean, when we lived in Tennessee, he was playing tackle football in kindergarten or first grade. And even at Michigan State, he said 'It's hard going to the football games and watching. I feel I like I should be out there.'"

Not that there weren't some scary moments, out there. Satterfield remembers one play in particular where Harris was hit in mid-air, turned sideways and flipped. It made him cringe—until, that is, Harris got up and went on his way.

"You just sit there and hope he's OK," Satterfield says. "But I knew he was a special player, so it didn't really bother me.

"And at the same time … I think the skill set he developed on the court he used on the football field, and the competitiveness and the strength and physicality of football helped him on the basketball floor."

And in the end, the basketball floor won out. His heart belonged to his mother's game—and his legend rested there, too.

The Shot

Brian Satterfield doesn't remember the exact date, season or circumstance. All he knows is that it was a close game and Hamilton Southeastern needed someone to step up.

Enter Gary Harris.

"We called timeout, diagrammed a play and tried to get it to him, let him take over," Satterfield says. "He did his thing. And he could do that at times. He knew if he needed to take over."

He knew it, certainly, the night of February 29, 2012, the first night of sectionals, with Hamilton Southeastern locked up in an 83-83 tie with North Central with 4.6 seconds to play. The Royals were inbounding the ball at midcourt. Harris came off a screen to the ball, dribbled right around one defender, spun back to his left away from a second defender, and launched a shot from straightaway, four or five strides across midcourt.

The 35-footer banked in just ahead of the horn. Pandemonium ensued. The Shot became an internet sensation, winding up on ESPN's Top Ten Plays of the Day and on websites as far afield as *The Huffington Post*.

It was also only one facet of his game that made him special, according to his coach.

"You know when he came here, everybody was talking about him being a freshman, the things he could do," Satterfield says. "But what separated him from a lot of the players who went through here and could have played earlier was what he could do at the defensive end.

"He is such a special defender. One, he uses his body well and understands angles, but he probably has the strongest hands I've ever seen. There would be so many

A couple of the youth coaches were players at Fishers. Recognizing the senior Harris, they indulged in a little trash-talking, tell him what they were going to do on Friday night to his son.

Harris came home steaming.

"'Are you ready for tomorrow?" he demanded of his son, who was sitting at the kitchen table with his mom.

"Yeah," Gary replied.

"No! Are you ready for tomorrow?" the senior Harris said again.

"Yeah," Gary replied again.

Not emphatic enough for his dad, who was still worked up.

"Do you know what those boys over there at Fishers are saying?" he went on. "They're saying they're gonna give you the business! They're saying they're gonna whip you bad! What you got to say about that?"

His son merely shrugged.

"We'll see tomorrow," he said.

"Never changed his expression," recalls Joy Harris.

And Friday night?

Hamilton Southeastern won 40-17. And Harris, as best his mom can recollect "had like five touchdowns."

"He's not one to talk and trash-talk and say 'We're gonna do this, and we're gonna do that'," she went on. "He just went out there quietly and did what needed to be done."

In truth, that's been his personality for as long as his parents and coaches can remember. Far more his mom's child than his dad's in that regard, he tends to low-key everything—to the point that, when he made the varsity as a freshman at Hamilton Southeastern, he didn't even tell his parents.

times in high school where guys would drive by somebo
else, and he would be over there in the gap and instead
knocking it away, he just reaches in there and grabs it a
takes off."

A shattering dunk at the other end usually punctua
the sequence. Or, just as likely, a deft assist out of a doul
team.

"He was never one to try to demand the bal
Satterfield says. "He's gonna find the open guy."

And without an abundance of fanfare. It was
another aspect of Harris' game, one that revealed itself
the video of The Shot: As soon as it banked in, the came
could no longer find its author, because Harris immedia
ly turned and, without ceremony, simply ran off the cou

Par for the course, his coach says, for a kid who is
undemonstrative as he is routinely spectacular.

"When he's out there on the court, out of the fo
years he was here, I'd say once he appeared to get a lit
rattled," Satterfield says. "He's always tried to be eve
keeled—not let the good times get to him too much, n
let the bad times get to him too much."

Doing What Needs To Be Done

The story goes like this: One day during Gary's juni
year, his dad came home from coaching the Harris's mid
dle son, Cameron, in youth football. It was the week
the big football showdown between Fishers and Hamilto
Southeastern, located not more than five miles apa
among the upscale neighborhoods and additions nort
and east of Indianapolis.

All he said was that he'd made the team, and then informed his mother that he needed a shirt and tie for the team picture.

A call or two to some of his friends' parents, however, produced a mystery: None of them knew anything about a team picture. Of course, none of their sons had made the varsity team, either. And only the varsity, one of the parents finally told Joy Harris, was getting its picture taken.

"You made the varsity? Why didn't you tell me?" Joy asked her son.

Again, he just shrugged.

"I remember thinking, 'Should he be on the varsity team? It's not gonna do him any good if he's gonna sit the bench. Put him back on the JV or put him back on freshman team so he can play and continue to get better," Joy Harris says. "I was really concerned.

"And the first game I said, 'OK, I think he can play varsity.'"

Even if he didn't think it was worth mentioning.

"It's funny," Joy Harris says. "People ask me all the time, 'I just don't know what he's thinking sometimes.' That's the thing with Gary. It takes him some time to warm up to people. But once he does, he has a great sense of humor. He's real even-keeled, doesn't get too high or too low off of things."

The Little Things

For all of Harris' exploits, Hamilton Southeastern won just one sectional during his time there. It was in his junior year, when Harris averaged 18.6 points 5.0 rebounds, 3.0

assists and 2.7 steals for a Royals squad that went 20-4 and reached the Class 4A regional finals before losing to North Central.

Along the way, they won only the second sectional in school history, beating rival Carmel 57-53 in the championship game.

That isn't what stands out for Brian Satterfield, however.

What stands out is one moment during the game when Harris got knocked off balance sailing in for a layoff and tumbled into the stands, landing on a little kid.

"After we win the sectional, of course we're all celebrating," Satterfield says. "Not Gary. He's going over there to check on the kid to make sure he's OK.

"I mean, it's just little things like that with him. He's always been willing to give back. He's always been willing to give his time. If somebody had a little birthday party for their kid, we'd do something in the gym where he'd be the highlight and just doing stuff to work with them. It makes their day. He was always willing to do that stuff.

"That's Gary Harris."

* * *

Gary Harris's gift for standing out didn't end with the 35-foot shot in high school that wound up as an ESPN Play of the Day, nor his 2012 Mr. Basketball accolade, nor his Big Ten Freshman of the Year season at Michigan State when he was eighteen years old.

It continues.

At Michigan State, he was even better his sophomore year, averaging 16.7 points and 4.1 rebounds and becoming one of the Spartans' go-to offensive threats. At the end of the season, he declared for the 2014 NBA draft, where the Chicago Bulls took him with the 19th pick in the first round.

Traded to Denver, he averaged 13.1 minutes and 3.4 points his rookie year. But as at Michigan State, his numbers have gone up every year since.

In 2016–17, the 6-foot-4, 210-pound Harris averaged 31.3 minutes, 3.1 rebounds, and 2.9 assists. His .420 shooting percentage from the 3-point line ranked him 8th in the NBA.

CHAPTER 8

MISCELLANEOUS

A League of Their Own

Crawfordsville won the Indiana High School Athletic Association's first state championship, which was staged March 10-11, 1911 at Indiana University.

While the Athenians' victory is common knowledge among Indiana high school boys' basketball historians, many Hoosiers have no idea that from 1928 through 1942, this state's Catholic high schools staged their own state tournament.

That's because until August 15, 1942, parochial high schools were not allowed to apply for Indiana High School Athletic Association membership.

Indianapolis Cathedral won Catholic state championships in 1928, 1929, 1932 and 1933. Decatur Catholic was the 1930 winner, followed by Washington St. Simon in 1931.

Huntington Catholic, Anderson St. Mary, Fort Wayne Central Catholic and Evansville Memorial were the other parochial champions. Fort Wayne Central Catholic won the final parochial tournament in 1942.

Beginning with the 1943 state tournament through 1997, no parochial school ever won Indiana's single-class boys' basketball state tournament.

Indianapolis Brebeuf came close in 1991 but was beaten by Glenn Robinson-led Gary Roosevelt in the state championship game in the RCA Dome.

In the very first year of the four-class tournament, Indianapolis Cathedral won the 1998 Class 3A state championship, and Lafayette Central Catholic won the Class A title.

Lafayette Central Catholic won three Class A titles during the first seven years of the multiple-class tournament system and was runner-up in another.

One Tough Act

There's something to be said for an athletic team that is hungry while at the same time carries a chip on its shoulders.

To say those statements applied to the East Chicago Washington basketball team of 1960 would be an understatement.

From mid-October—when basketball practice began—until the end of March when Indiana's finest four teams gathered in Hinkle Fieldhouse to determine a state champion—coach John Baratto's team heard a steady stream of dialogue centered on Muncie Central.

Muncie Central. Muncie Central. Muncie Central.

To be frank, the Senators were so sick and tired of hearing about how talented the Ron Bonham-led Bearcats were that they decided to take matters into their own strong hands.

Literally.

While Bonham and his Muncie Central teammates were destroying everything in their path on the way to the 1960 state championship game, East Chicago Washington was fighting for its basketball life in talent-rich Lake County, where hard-working steel workers taught their children the value of a dollar and the value of refusing to lose without a fight.

East Chicago Washington lost regular-season games to Gary Roosevelt and to Gary Tolleston, but the Senators' mission was established.

Led by gritty guard Bob Cantrell, tough center Jim Bakos, smooth forward Phil Dawkins and hard-nosed forward Ron Divjak, Baratto's team was prepared for a street fight if one was needed.

After all, not far from East Chicago Washington High School was a hair-styling salon with the name "Curl Up and Dye." Now, that's a tough neighborhood.

While they certainly grew into gentlemen, most of the Senators were reared in tough neighborhoods.

In other parts of the state, opponents were backing down from powerful Muncie Central. All East Chicago Washington wanted was an opportunity to play 32 minutes against what most considered one of the greatest teams in Indiana schoolboy history.

The Senators took the all-important first step by winning the East Chicago sectional, which included a very difficult 54-50 first-round victory against Hammond Tech.

In the East Chicago regional, the Senators manhandled Valparaiso by 19 points and then avenged a regular-season loss to Gary Roosevelt with a thrilling 60-58 triumph.

Traveling south to Lafayette for the semistate at Purdue, East Chicago Washington was on a roll. The Senators eased past Logansport 66-59, then routed tiny Covington 77-51 in the Lafayette semistate's championship game.

In Indianapolis, the two Final Four semifinal games were as different as night and day. In the opener, Muncie Central destroyed Bloomington 102-66, getting 40 points from Bonham.

East Chicago Washington had to dig deep for a 62-61 victory against Fort Wayne Central, getting 15 points from Cantrell and 12 each from Divjak and Dawkins.

Now, the Senators had their wish—one shot at Muncie Central.

Most were so impressed by the Bearcats' 36-point drubbing of a good Bloomington team in the opening semifinal that it was believed Muncie Central would do the same to Baratto's tough guys.

What happened that March night in 1960 still is shocking to many in Muncie, and a sense of great pride for those who live in East Chicago.

Bonham scored 25 for the state's No. 1-ranked team, but East Chicago Washington never backed away from the opening tip, recording a 75-59 victory.

Dawkins led the way with 21 points, center Bakos added 17 and Cantrell ran the show with 11 points and lots of assists.

After the game, Cantrell received the Indiana High School Athletic Association's Trester Award for scholarship, citizenship and athletic ability. From there, Cantrell accepted a basketball scholarship from Michigan coach Dave Strack and was the Wolverines' starting point guard for three seasons, playing with the great Cazzie Russell.

Dawkins went on to Purdue, where he enjoyed an excellent career playing for coach Ray Eddy.

Student manager Frank Kollintzas even parlayed his role into a bright future in the community, eventually securing the athletic director's job at East Chicago Central—a consolidation of Washington and Roosevelt.

Cantrell returned to East Chicago and coach the basketball team in the late 1960s before becoming involved in school administration and local politics.

While it has been more than 40 years since the Senators made the most of the one shot they sought, their victory still is considered one of the most stunning upsets in Indiana title-game history.

Not so much because the Senators prevailed. Certainly, they were a talented team. But beating Bonham-led Muncie Central by 16 points took one very special effort from a collection of players who weren't impressed by what had been accomplished in the past.

East Chicago Washington was that team.

A Sports Writer's Prank

From time to time, Indiana basketball coaches take their sport—and themselves—a bit too seriously.

As Lafayette Jeff's Jack Schult learned during a 1966 junior varsity game, leave it to a free-spirited sports writer to supply a humorous dose of reality.

Schult, who coached the Bronchos' boys' tennis team to Indiana's 1975 state championship, was a novice basketball coach during the mid-1960s.

The locker rooms at the former Jeff gym on Lafayette's North Ninth Street were located in the school's basement, which was a popular halftime gathering place for school officials and media members.

Now-deceased former *Journal and Courier* sports writer Dick Ham often would visit the basement for a halftime cup of coffee and a cigarette.

Ham was amused by the serious nature of the Bronchos' then-young JV coach, often teasing the likeable Schult, who had bit acting roles in the movies *Hoosiers* and *Eight Men Out.*

On a chilly Friday night in January, 1966, Ham was standing outside the Jeff locker room as Schult delivered an inspiring halftime speech, which was intended to help the JV team rally from a small deficit.

As Ham listened to Schult's speech, he decided to pull a prank. As the players filed out of the locker room, Ham waited for the perfect moment, then pulled the bolted door shut, locking Schult inside.

"I had just finished talking, and the kids headed upstairs," Schult recalled. "Out of habit, I combed my hair and adjusted my tie before following the team back onto the court. I heard the door shut, and as I attempted to open it, I realized it was locked from the outside.

"Well, I couldn't get out. Fortunately, there was an intercom system from the locker room to the athletic office. I yelled for someone to come unlock the door, and fortunately, they responded. One of the custodians unlocked the door. By the time I got back upstairs, the second half had begun, and we had taken the lead."

Jeff pulled away for an easy victory.

"For years to come, every time I saw Dick Ham, he reminded me that he should be credited for that coaching win," Schult said. "He would say, 'You got them behind in the first half, so I just made sure they would have a chance to win before you messed them up any more.'

"I coached football, basketball, baseball and tennis during my career, and I've seen a lot of crazy things in sports, but that's absolutely the wildest prank I've heard of, and it happened to me."

Ham, a World War II veteran, covered every Indiana boys' basketball state finals from 1948 through 1976. A West Lafayette graduate, Ham's first state finals assignment included a twist of irony—Marion Crawley-coached Lafayette Jeff won it.

Pine Village Playground

Tuesdays. Always Tuesdays.

For budding young high school basketball standouts in Benton and Warren counties, summer Tuesday nights were reserved for the outdoor court games at Pine Village High School, now a part of the Seeger Memorial consolidation.

Most Tuesday night participants were products of farm communities such as Oxford, Otterbein, Fowler, Templeton, Earl Park, Williamsport, and of course, Pine Village.

During June, July and August of 1971, the Tuesday night action was so intense that it rivaled the emotion of any sectional championship game.

The Pine Village kids took ownership of these Tuesday roundball extravaganzas. Joe Howarth was the enforcer. The muscle man. The guy who denied the lane to any Benton County kid who dared attempt that path to the basket.

Terry Lemming was the friendly, talented guard who liked everybody—teammate or opponent. Then there was the Pine Village star—6-foot-5 Bax Brutus, whose wingspan, leaping ability and nose for the ball near the goal made him the one to watch.

Dan Dawson led the Benton County group. Strong. Physical. Rugged rebounder. Never saw a shot he didn't like. Dawson, then a senior-to-be at Benton Central, couldn't wait for the two and a half-hour sessions on the smooth Pine Village court, which featured the old-fashioned, fan-shaped bankboards.

Dawson would practice by himself at Otterbein in preparation for the games against the Pine Village guys, who attended a school whose four-grade enrollment was 160.

In 1971-72, Benton Central's enrollment was 10 times that of Pine Village.

The schools were located only eight miles apart. Some farms of Benton Central kids bordered the farms of those who attended Pine Village.

Purdue vs. Indiana. Alabama vs. Auburn. Duke vs. North Carolina.

In rural, west-central Indiana, Benton Central vs. Pine Village was a mini-version of each rivalry.

"I was fortunate to average 21 points a game my senior year, and to this day, I tell people there are two reasons for that success," said Dawson, now athletic director at his alma mater. "No. 1, I played for a great high school coach in Dave Nicholson. No. 2, I played every Tuesday night in the summer at Pine Village."

Dawson and Lemming became such good friends that Dawson was best man in Lemming's wedding. Even today, Dawson claims Howarth is among the best small-school defenders he's ever seen.

And Brutus? Well, sadly, the world never got to enjoy the real Bax Brutus.

After the 1971-72 school year, Brutus was electrocuted in a tragic farming accident. He would have been a Pine Village senior at the time of his death.

But the summer games of 1971 served as an appetizer for the 1971-72 state tournament series.

Throughout Dawson's senior year at Benton Central, which was Brutus's junior year at Pine Village, the rivalry intensified when Pine Village coach Bill Barrett told media members that Benton Central refused to schedule his team.

Then, each team won its sectional, advancing to the Lafayette regional, where Pine Village and Benton Central were matched in the first semifinal.

In front of a crowd of more than 6,000, the kids who had honed their skills seven months before in the summer heat of Indiana squared off in a regional game for the ages.

"I've played a lot of basketball, coached a lot of basketball and been the athletic director for a lot of basketball, and I've never participated nor seen a game with that kind of intensity," Dawson said.

"For 32 minutes, nobody slacked off for a single possession. Nobody let his opponent have an easy look at the basket. Everybody earned every point he scored."

The lead changed hands early and often, but Dawson and Benton Central took advantage of information about Brutus that had been learned on the summer court in Pine Village.

"Bax loved to lower his shoulder and turn to his left as he approached the basket," Dawson said. "I moved his way each time he did that. By late in the fourth quarter, he fouled out with his fifth offensive foul. We got him for charging five times."

In limited minutes, Brutus found a way to score 23 points. Dawson fouled out with 22, but Benton Central prevailed, 71-69.

It was a very emotional victory for Dawson. His mother, the former Lois Pearson, is a Pine Village High School graduate. His aunt, Jonora Pearson, was the Pine Village school nurse.

And Dawson's uncle, Bowater Pearson, claimed to be Pine Village's No. 1 fan.

"I doubt that in the last 50 years there's been a fan thrown out of more high school gyms than Bowater Pearson," Dawson said. "There are intense fans, and then there was my uncle Bowater."

From time to time, Dawson passes through Pine Village on his way to play golf at Big Pine Golf Course or at Harrison Hills in Attica. Each time, Dawson slows down a bit, glancing at the outdoor court that was his home away from home during the summer of 1971.

"It's not in good shape now, but it's still there," Dawson said. "If people could have seen those games. They were really something. They were great guys who loved to play basketball. It was about as good as it gets for me."

Dawson coached boys' basketball at Sheridan and at Seeger, coached the girls' team at Carroll (Carroll County), then moved into athletic administration at Carroll and now at Benton Central when his sons, Jay and Brock, began playing varsity sports.

"I've got lots of basketball-related memories, but my fondest are those hot summer nights in Pine Village," Dawson said. "For rural Indiana, that's what Hoosier Hysteria was, is and always will be all about."

A Title Game for the Ages

While some state championship games are devoid of high drama, Indiana's 1994 finale certainly was worth the price of admission.

The fireworks began early in the RCA Dome shootout between unbeaten Valparaiso and twice-beaten South Bend Clay.

Valparaiso featured the dynamic backcourt of Bryce Drew and Tim Bishop, while South Bend Clay was led by sharp-shooting sophomore Jaraan Cornell.

Four eight-minute quarters were not enough to settle this northern Indiana slugfest between two potent offensive-oriented powerhouses.

Valpo led by eight points with less than a minute to play, but Cornell took a perfect pass off an out-of-bounds play with just more than a second remaining and sank a game-tying three-pointer as time expired.

Clay carried its momentum into overtime against the tiring Vikings, finally pulling away for a 93-88 state championship clinching victory.

The offensive proficiency that night sent media members scurrying to locate a state finals record book.

In the end, the 181 combined points produced a title game record. South Bend Clay's 32-point fourth quarter was a championship game record for most points in a single period. Valparaiso's number of three-point attempts (30) and three-pointers made (10) shattered the former championship game record.

Bishop (35) and Drew (34) combined for 69 points—the most ever scored by two players from the same team in a championship game.

Cornell, who finished with 30 to lead South Bend Clay, went on to star for four seasons at Purdue, where he became the school's career leader for three-pointers made.

But Cornell never will forget what he achieved in the 1994 state championship game.

"I was young at the time, but that really was a great game," Cornell said.

"The shot at the end of regulation was instinct more than anything. I didn't have time to think about it or worry about it, which probably helped me make it.

"We were behind most of the way, but we never thought we were out of it.

"We just kept playing—one possession at a time."

Drew went on to star at Valparaiso University, playing for his father Homer, and played in the NBA with Houston, Chicago, Charlotte and New Orleans. He returned to Valparaiso in 2005 as an assistant coach until his father's retirement, before becoming the team's head coach in 2011. He left Valpo for Vanderbilt's head coaching job in 2016.

Sadly, Bishop was killed in an automobile accident after beginning a career in professional baseball.